How to Develop a Powerful Prayer Life

The Biblical Path to Holiness and Relationship with God

*How to let Christ pray through you
and change the world!*

Dr. Gregory R. Frizzell

How to Develop a Powerful Prayer Life
ISBN 1-930285-00-0

Copyright © 1999 by Gregory R. Frizzell
Edited by K N Rowland
Cover Design by S Faithe Finley
Published by The Master Design
    in cooperation with Master Design Ministries
PO Box 17865
Memphis, TN 38187-0865
Info@masterdesign.org
www.masterdesign.org

Unless otherwise noted, Scripture quotations are from the KING JAMES VERSION AV of the Bible © 1973, Thomas Nelson, Inc., Publishers.

Printed by Bethany Press International in the USA.

JJ

Other Books by Gregory R. Frizzell

- Returning to Holiness: A Personal and Churchwide Journey to Revival
- Prayer Evangelism for the Local Church: *"One Church's Miraculous Story of Blessing and Deliverance"*
- Local Associations and United Prayer: *Keys to the Coming Revival*
- Biblical Patterns for Powerful Church Prayer Meetings
- Statewide Prayer Strategies: *"Biblical Patterns for Spiritual Awakening"*
- A Five Year Associational Vision Based on 2 Chronicles 7:14
- National Strategies for Powerful United Prayer
- Pastors' Prayer Meetings: *"Journey to Areawide Revival"*
- Training Deacons for Crisis Counseling
- How to Develop an Evangelistic Church Prayer Ministry

Church and Areawide Conferences by Gregory R. Frizzell

- Developing a Powerful Personal Prayer Life
- Developing a Powerful Church Prayer Meeting
- Comprehensive Strategies for Prayer Evangelism
- Developing Powerful Corporate Prayer Meetings
- Toward Revival and Spiritual Awakening in Our Day
- Solemn Assemblies for Churches and Associations
- Concerts of Prayer and Worship

To schedule a conference or order books contact:

Dr. Gregory R Frizzell
3759 N. Watkins
Memphis, TN 38127

901.357.5333
gfrizzell@earthlink.net

Table of Contents

Introduction

Powerful Prayer is for Every Believer

Prayer is the heart and soul of every successful relationship with God. In fact, prayer is absolutely crucial to every area of a believer's life. To illustrate the point, consider the following questions. How did you receive Christ as your Lord and Savior? How do you abide in Christ and allow Him to live His life through you? How do you grow as a Christian? How do you overcome temptation and weakness? How do you resist Satan and wage effective spiritual warfare? How do you confess your sins? How are you filled with the Holy Spirit? How do you obtain guidance and wisdom from God? How do you experience the power to serve God effectively? *The answer to every single question is prayer!* Indeed, prayer is essential to every part of our relationship with God (John 15:7).

In view of the awesome importance of prayer, I confidently make the following statement. "No one's relationship with Christ will ever rise above the level of his or her praying." Put simply, if your prayer life is inconsistent and weak, so will be your relationship with God! But take heart, dear friend, you *can* develop a dynamic prayer life! And when you learn to walk in powerful daily prayer, God will transform your entire life.

Though powerful prayer is certainly God's will for every believer, studies show most believers feel very inadequate about their prayer life. Or worse yet, a believer may think he has a good prayer life when according to the biblical definition of prayer, that is simply not the case. Tragically, many modern believers have little idea what constitutes a truly effective prayer life. In this book, our purpose is to help every Christian fully understand and experience a dynamic prayer life. Toward that purpose, you will experience five results as you seek God through these pages.

- You will gain a clear understanding of prayer
  from God's perspective and purpose.

- You will discover a full biblical understanding of what constitutes a powerful prayer life.
- You will learn how to let Christ become the very source and power of your prayer life.
- You will experience new motivation and confidence to develop a dynamic prayer life.
- You will embrace a practical biblical pattern for developing powerful prayer and a dynamic personal relationship with Christ.

Because we live in a busy day of sound bites and micromanaged time slots, many believers have begun to approach prayer in a rushed, highly programmed manner. Yet God is definitely calling His people back to the biblical pattern of significant time with Him through daily prayer. He is calling us back to dynamic spiritual cleansing and an intimate walk with Himself. *This book is designed to show you how to experience the mighty fullness of God through daily prayer.* It is my earnest prayer that God will give you both the desire and ability to move out of the shallows and into the glorious depths of relationship with Christ.

Learning to View Prayer from God's Perspective

My deepest prayer is for believers to learn to view prayer from God's perspective. In fact, we will never fully understand prayer until we grasp God's primary *purposes* for prayer. We must stop viewing prayer merely as a means to get our needs met. Far more than just meeting needs, prayer is God's primary means of our coming to know Him, worship Him and experience transformation through the indwelling Christ. As Christians, we are called the very Bride of Christ (Revelation 21:9). Through prayer and Scripture, God is preparing us for the great wedding soon to come. He is readying us to rule and reign with Him forever (Revelation 22:5).

Friend, prayer is not primarily about what we can get out of God, but what He purposes to do in and through us for His own pleasure. Prayer is a major way we come to know Him and hear His voice. Through prayer, we abide in Him and allow Him to live through us. Prayer is how Christ purifies His Bride and builds His Kingdom. The great secret of prayer is to align ourselves to God's purposes rather than seeking to align Him to ours. In the coming pages, you will see how this can be done through God's enabling grace!

Before I describe the essential steps to a God-focused prayer life, it is important to grasp the full scope of all you will gain from dynamic prayer. Until you are totally convinced of the importance of a lifestyle of prayer, you are not likely to take the necessary steps to achieve one. Carefully consider eight God-ordained results of a powerful, biblical prayer life.

What God Wants You to Gain Through Effective Prayer

1. **Your relationship with Him will become much more real and personal.** Scriptures declare that a believer's greatest priority is to personally know God and love Him with all his heart (Matthew 22:37, John 17:3). Above everything else, God desires a close personal relationship with each of His children. Yet, it is *impossible* to develop this relationship without spending significant time with God. Prayer is the primary way you spend meaningful time with the Savior. Through prayer, God purposes to establish and deepen your personal relationship with Him.

2. **You will experience ever-deepening holiness and life transforming discipleship.** Today, we hear much of the phrase "life-transforming discipleship." Yet, there is no such thing as life-transforming discipleship that is not centered on significant time in fervent prayer and Scripture reading. Friend, if you will learn to spend significant time in prayer and Scripture, you will experience discipleship in a way that is utterly miraculous! Through this type of prayer life, God will radically fill you with His own holiness, purity and character.

3. **Your ability to clearly hear God's voice will rise dramatically** (James 1:5, Jeremiah 29:13). God promises clear direction and wisdom to those who seriously seek His direction. Jesus said His sheep would *hear* and know His voice (John 10:27). To put it simply, if a believer consistently seeks God's face, he finds Him! Unless you spend significant time in regular prayer, God's voice will be difficult to discern. Without much time in regular prayer, you will be spiritually "hard of hearing" and God will often seem distant.

4. **The spiritual power of your life and ministry will increase greatly** (John 14:12-14; Acts 1:8). Where there is little prayer, there is little power. Conversely, where there is much prayer, there is much power. Unfortunately, many people are excellent organizers, good promoters, and brilliant strategists, but few are powerful prayer warriors. Thus in effect, we have totally *reversed* the practice and priority of the early church. We do everything else far more than we pray, while the New Testament church prayed far more than they did anything else! Consequently, the early church rapidly evangelized their world, while our baptism ratios have been in an alarming fifty year decline.

5. **You will experience a dramatic increase in answered prayer** (John 15:7). When believers truly abide in Christ, their prayers take on far greater power and effectiveness. You will notice many more answers to your prayers. It is *only* through the constant cleansing and filling of God's Spirit that our prayers have mountain-moving power. Conversely, it is *only* through much time in prayer that we maintain the total cleansing and filling of the Holy Spirit. Failure to spend adequate time in "confession and cleansing" is the primary reason many believers see few answered prayers (Psalms 66:18; Isaiah 59:1-2).

6. **You will experience far greater power to withstand trials, temptations, and spiritual attacks** (2 Corinthians 10:3-5). Prayer is the primary way we put on the whole armor of God.

It is the essential way we wage spiritual warfare. When our prayer life is weak or inconsistent, our spiritual defenses are down. The more consistently one prays, the greater will be his ability to overcome the world, the flesh, and the devil. The less one prays, the greater his vulnerability to sin, Satan and worldliness.

7. **As you learn to effectively pray for the lost, you will see many people saved.** Every believer can learn how to pray effectively for the lost and backslidden. As you make time for prayer, God will lead you in how to develop a lost prayer list and see dozens saved from your list. When you learn to pray in this manner, you will also see a mighty increase in the numbers saved in your church. In this fashion, your prayers will have a powerful impact on your church and your entire city! You will see many precious friends and loved ones brought to Christ. Through prayer, God will use you in powerful evangelism and missions.

8. **You will discover how to pray effectively for revival and spiritual awakening in your church, city, and nation** (Ezekiel 22:30). Though most believers are burdened for America, few know how to intercede effectively for our land. As you develop a biblical prayer life, you will discover how to pray specific prayers for your church and nation. When your prayers become *biblical* and *specific*, they take on far greater power. You will discover how your personal prayers can make an awesome difference in the spiritual condition of your church, city and nation. Rather than feeling helpless, you will see your prayers take on a powerful new authority. Indeed, the whole world is impacted when ordinary believers become powerful intercessors. Spiritually, no nation rises above the collective prayer practice of God's people.

Though I could easily list many other benefits of prayer, these eight are some of the most important. Beyond question, a powerful prayer life will revolutionize your relationship with God! *To a large degree, your prayer life is your relationship with God.*

So friend, we now come to two crucial questions: Are you ready to begin a powerful new relationship with God? Do you truly hunger for a deeper spiritual filling and vibrant new life and ministry? Believer, I want to assure you that God is ready to touch your life. No matter how much you've struggled in the past, you can experience a powerful prayer life!

A Testimony of God's Grace Through Prayer

After salvation, my greatest spiritual decision came when I was 16 years of age. I had just been called to preach and felt quite overwhelmed by the call. By nature I was somewhat quiet and thought God had surely made a mistake in calling me into the ministry. In order to find encouragement, I began a study of the lives of powerful preachers and missionaries. I also did thorough research into the great revivals and spiritual awakenings of history. As I studied and prayed, I noticed a distinct common denominator in the lives of all great saints and in every Great Awakening. That common denominator was the practice of spending **much** time in daily prayer and Bible reading!

It began to dawn on me that God mightily uses even the weakest believers who spend serious time in fervent daily prayer (1 Corinthians 1:26). In my study, it became obvious that God most uses *very ordinary* people who learn to abide in Christ through serious daily prayer (John 15:4). I saw that everything revolves around a close prayer relationship with Jesus Christ!

I will never forget the night in my parents' backyard, when in desperation, I asked God how I could ever become an effective minister. That night God spoke so clearly that I have never been the same. His message was simple: "*If you will spend much time with me in close relationship and prayer, you will never lack for my mighty presence and miraculous power.*" God used John 15:5 and 2 Corinthians 3:4-6 to drive this truth deep into my heart.

By God's grace, I committed to make significant daily prayer my top priority. Though I could certainly never claim perfection in my prayer life, as a 16 year-old, the habit of significant daily prayer became the major pattern of my life. Through the years, that one practice has meant infinitely more than any other factor in my life! Even if I could earn a thousand doctorate degrees, they would never impact me like significant daily time with Jesus.

I could write a huge book just describing the miracles that have sprung directly from my simple daily prayer time. My heart floods with joy as I think of a nationwide ministry God has initiated solely through prayer. I am astounded at the impossible obstacles and trials God has overcome through daily prayer.

My friend, I share this testimony for one reason. *To show God's mighty grace through simple relational prayer.* Believe me, if I can see God's grace through prayer, you can too! No matter how big or little your task, no matter how devastating your problems, significant daily prayer is the absolute key to a miraculous new walk with Christ!

Please Don't Sell Yourself Short

I want to shout from the housetops that powerful prayer is God's will for every believer! Dear believer, it is essential that you get the vision to go beyond a three or four minute daily devotion! Please believe that you do not have to be a pastor or spend two or three hours a day to experience a dynamic prayer life. If you will give only 30 to 45 minutes a day, that is certainly enough to experience miraculous new growth and ministry. Through Christ, you really can do this (Philippians 4:13).

Christian, it is time for us to "grow up" as disciples of Jesus Christ. Our nation is in desperate need of another Great Awakening, yet it can only come if ordinary believers commit to serious time in prayer. You will never experience full power and growth until you make significant time for daily prayer. Please stop settling for a shallow walk with Christ when God saved you to experience all the fullness of His daily presence.

A Special Word to Pastors and Christian Workers

Today it is utterly tragic that many pastors and leaders indicate such little time in serious prayer. In fact, modern surveys reveal a marked difference between the prayer life of today's pastor and the pastors of past Great Awakenings. It seems that today's busy leaders have bought into the unbiblical notion that all you need is a "brief daily devotion." Yet, biblically and historically, *nothing* could be further from the truth! There is simply no shortcut to a dynamic walk with Christ or to the mountain-moving power of the Holy Spirit.

While most Christian leaders place huge emphasis on programs and promotion, surveys show that few spend major time in daily prayer and spiritual cleansing. Today it is rare to find pastors or Christian leaders who are true giants of personal prayer. That is especially sobering since churches seldom become powerhouses of prayer until their pastors are men of prayer. If America is to see another Great Awakening, pastors must once again become men of mountain-moving prayer. Praise God for growing signs that at last, this is beginning to happen!

After pastoring for 16 years in a highly transitional gang-ridden area, I *know* how God uses serious biblical prayer. Though I have had countless opportunities to leave for much easier churches, God instructed me to stay in order to show His power in a most impossible setting. Christian leader, no matter what you are facing, God will bring revolutionary changes *if* you embrace genuine biblical prayer. Mark this well — dynamic new life and ministry awaits *everyone* who draws near to God in powerful daily prayer (Matthew 7:7).

How to Meet God Through This Book

This book is designed to be used by the youngest believer or the most mature saint. While its biblical principles challenge and instruct the most seasoned prayer warrior, it is simply written to lead the youngest believer into dynamic prayer and spiritual growth. It is not written just to convey information, but to lead you on a relationship prayer journey with God. Through these pages, God is going to challenge and call you to a far deeper relationship with Himself.

As you read this book, pay special attention to the study questions and sample prayers at the end of each section. Above all, spend time talking to God about the things He reveals in each chapter. Remember friend, you won't learn to pray by merely "reading" about prayer. You will learn to pray by "praying" about the things you read. Be sure to make time to encounter God at the end of each chapter. I further encourage you to record answers to the study questions in a prayer journal instead of this book so you will not be limited by space.

In Chapter One, we will explore the three essential foundations upon which to build your prayer relationship with God. In Chapter Two, I will explain the five basic *types* of prayer. In Chapters Three through Eight, I will teach you to experience all five elements so essential to powerful daily prayer. The majority of the book is given to a clear explanation of each element. This book is designed to give you a practical handle for experiencing all five types of prayer in your daily relationship with God. The final chapter is a practical guide and pattern for use in your daily prayer life.

Above all, remember that prayer is a *relationship* with Jesus Christ! Before you read any further, please pause and ask God to revolutionize your walk with Him. That's one prayer God will answer every time!

Toward the Next Great Awakening,

Gregory R. Frizzell

Questions for Discussion and Reflection

1. Name several key blessings we receive from God through prayer.

2. In your own words, describe why prayer is so vital to every area of your life and relationship to God.

3. What do you think it means to pray from God's perspective rather than a selfish perspective?

4. In your own words, briefly describe God's eight purposes for your prayer life.

5. Do you think God has called you to experience a powerful prayer life? Why or why not?

Prayers for Daily Growth

* Father, I ask You to fill me with a passion to know You and love You with all my heart (Matthew 22:37). Lord, teach me to view prayer as the heart of our relationship (Luke 11:1). Please enable me to hear Your voice and pray in the center of Your will (1 John 5:14-15).

* Dear Lord, teach me to pray from Your perspective and will, not my own (Mark 14:36). Open my eyes to the revelation of Your great purposes for my life.

* God, please speak to me and grant me ears to clearly hear Your voice (Isaiah 30:21). Grant me the desire to be holy because You are holy. Fill me with genuine worship and help me worship You in ways truly pleasing to You (John 4:23). God, help me pray not just to get "blessed," but because I truly love You (James 4:2).

* Lord, teach me to die to myself and to trust Christ to live through me (Galatians 2:20). Baptize me in Your mighty power and anoint my spiritual gifts to Your service (Acts 1:8). Fill me with Your passion for souls and help me witness to all who cross my path.

Chapter One

*Understanding the Three Foundations
of a Powerful Prayer Life*

If you are to experience a powerful prayer life, you must first establish a solid prayer foundation. Any builder knows that a structure is never stronger than its foundation. No building can stand long without a strong foundation and the same truth applies to developing a prayer life. In order to build a consistent, biblical prayer life, you must approach it from the right foundation. Without strong prayer foundations, your relationship with Christ will be weak and inconsistent.

In this chapter, we examine three foundations absolutely essential to powerful prayer and life-changing discipleship. These foundations are not only vital for prayer, they are crucial to your whole walk with Christ. Remember, when we speak of your prayer life, we are not talking about an activity or discipline, *we are talking about the very heart of your relationship to Christ!* Before you study the three prayer foundations, pause and ask God to help you honestly evaluate your daily level of prayer.

First Foundation of a Powerful Prayer Life:

You must view your daily prayer time as a relationship with God and not some legalistic duty or discipline.

It is important to note that the Pharisees spent much time in regular prayer and fasting yet, they had no personal relationship with God. A powerful prayer life is not just a discipline or ritual, it is your commitment to a personal relationship with God. From God's perspective, prayer is the expression of that which He desires most — your personal relationship of love, surrender and trust. Prayer must be viewed as your commitment to spend meaningful time in personal relationship with the living God. John 17:3: "And this is life eternal, that they might *know* thee, the only true God, and Jesus Christ whom thou hast sent."

It is amazing that we put so much emphasis on serving and working *for* God when above all He wants our heartfelt personal love. Matthew 22:37: "You shall love the Lord your God with all your heart, with all your soul, and with all your mind." In 1 Corinthians 13:1-3, Paul further states that sacrifice and service are meaningless if they do not proceed from a genuine love relationship.

Allow me to illustrate this important point: when you were dating your spouse, did you ever say, "Honey you're important to me and because you are, I'm going to try and give you five whole minutes each day!" Or, did you ever say, "Honey it's just so hard for me to spend time with you, but I'm going to force myself to do it a few minutes each week!" Friend, if you ever did say such things, I know one thing for sure. That person would never have married you! But why do such statements sound so absurd? It's very simple. When you truly love someone, you want to spend as much time with them as possible. If you love someone, the close relationship is a joy, not a duty! In some ways, love for God is spelled T-I-M-E. If you truly love God, time with Him is your greatest joy.

How do you think it makes God feel when you make little or no time to be alone with Him? What does it say to God when you say, "It's so hard for me to make any serious time for prayer and Bible reading"? When you make such statements, you are saying loud and clear, "God, I don't love you, and I don't want to spend time with you." It tells God that you are not committed to developing your personal relationship with Him. (Remember, actions speak much louder than words.)

Especially in today's busy society, we must relearn the crucial lesson of Luke 10:38-43. In this story, Martha and Mary were two sisters with very different views of what mattered to God. Martha was busy doing all kinds of tasks *for* Jesus but had no time to just to fellowship *with* Him. Yet, Mary put her first priority on making time to sit quietly in His presence and listen. After a while,

Martha approached Jesus and asked Him to rebuke Mary for being lazy. Much to her surprise, Jesus rebuked Martha and stated that Mary had chosen the "better part" that would not be taken from her. This story contains a truth of enormous importance! We need much time with God before we attempt work *for* God.

Tragically, most believers are more like busy Martha than prayerful Mary. We are so busy *for* God that we spend very little time *with* Him. Jesus is clearly saying that our first priority is to spend much time *with* Him. Only then can we love Him as He desires to be loved. In John 15:5, Jesus states that we can do *nothing* unless we maintain a very close relationship with Him. We can only maintain such a relationship by spending much time in regular prayer!

Friend, if you say you are too busy to spend serious time in daily prayer, you have missed the whole point of your relationship and service to God! God first wants you and only then does He want your service. *It is the love relationship He desires far above all the serving and tithing in the world.*

If you are to become a powerful intercessor and Christian, you must view your prayer time as a relationship and not a religious chore or legalistic requirement. Viewing prayer as a daily love relationship is the first foundation of a powerful prayer life!

Second Foundation of a Powerful Prayer Life:

You must make an absolute commitment to consistently spend significant time alone with God in uninterrupted prayer.

Perhaps the greatest hindrance to modern spirituality is the busy, hectic pace of today's society. Modern believers have tragically bought into the notion that a three or four minute daily "quiet time" constitutes a powerful prayer life. Yet biblically and historically, nothing could be further from the truth! Certainly there is an important place for brief momentary prayer devotions, but we must never think these can replace the "closet prayer" when we enter God's presence and shut out everything else.

Matthew 6:6: "But you, when you pray, enter into your closet, and when you have shut the door, pray to your Father which is in secret; and your Father which sees in secret shall reward you openly."

As we view the prayer practices of Jesus and New Testament believers, it is clear they regularly spent much time alone in fervent prayer. It is also clear that believers and churches of every Great Awakening averaged much more time praying than do we. When you study the lives of people mightily used of God, you find one great common denominator. *Almost without exception, God's greatest servants spent much time in fervent daily prayer!*

Brief, inconsistent prayer times never produce powerful Spirit-filled believers. Furthermore, brief inconsistent prayer never has and never will bring a Great Spiritual Awakening. In America, we have made a "god" of convenience and ease. We want to give God a brief minute or two and try to fit Him into our busy schedules if it is convenient. The God of the Universe deserves (and requires) far more than this to release His full power on our lives.

If Jesus and the early church spent much time in prayer, what makes us think we can do less? If every generation which saw a sweeping Great Awakening, spent much time in prayer, why would we think God has changed His requirement for today? God's requirements have not changed and they never will! Unfortunately, what has changed is our *definition* of what constitutes a powerful prayer life. My purpose in this book is to return believers to the essential biblical practice of significant time in daily prayer.

Let me again restate the second foundation in simple terms. *No believer can develop a truly powerful, biblical prayer life without regularly spending much time alone with God.* This is a foundational requirement and a changeless spiritual principle. Friend, until you personally settle this issue and commit to consistent time with God, you will never go to the fullest depths of prayer or spiritual maturity. But what does it really mean to make an "absolute commitment" to spend *significant* time alone with God? In the next few paragraphs, we will analyze this second foundation, phrase by phrase. We begin with the first phrase of this prayer foundation.

You must make an absolute commitment to consistently spend significant time alone with God in uninterrupted prayer.

The first phrase mentions the need for an "absolute commitment." This emphasizes that your prayer time is a major priority that you carefully schedule and guard. You plan for it and take steps to protect it. But why must your prayer commitment be so absolute? Consider three crucial reasons:

First Reason for Absolute Commitment - Satan fears intercession more than anything else and fights prayer like no other area of your life. He does so for the following reasons:

- Prayer is an essential piece of your arsenal of spiritual warfare (2 Corinthians 10:7). It is through prayer that all other weapons are used.
- Prayer is crucial to putting on the whole armor of God (Ephesians 6:10-17).
- Prayer is the primary way we exert spiritual authority and wage effective spiritual warfare (2 Corinthians 10:3-5; Ephesians 6:10-17).
- Prayer is crucial to true evangelism (Acts 2-4).
- Prayer is the central element of all great revivals and spiritual awakenings (along with Scripture) (2 Chronicles 7:14).

Since prayer and Scripture are your primary weapons, it is little wonder that Satan will do *anything* to keep you from praying consistently. He will also fight to keep you from *deepening* your prayer power. If he cannot keep you from praying, he will fight to keep you from praying *effectively*. If your commitment to prayer is not absolute, Satan will certainly pressure you out of its daily practice. He will cause you to "settle" for a shallow ineffective prayer life. Satan's ploy is to get you so busy with "good" things that you make little time for the "best." Has Satan been successful in your life?

Second Reason for Absolute Commitment - Our flesh always resists the development of a powerful prayer life.

The following Scriptures contain strong examples of the flesh hindering prayer and spiritual growth (Matthew 26:40 - 41, Romans 7:14-18). From these texts we see that serious prayer is often more like a spiritual battle than a brief moment of sweet reflection. Powerful intercession frequently involves intense spiritual labor and warfare. The demonic atmosphere of our very planet resists the praying saint. Our physical bodies and earthly passions resist the practice of fervent prayer.

A Personal Illustration

Upon entering seminary, I was taking many classes and working long hours. Despite my schedule, I knew God had called me to spend much time in daily prayer and Scripture study. To do this, I had to rise extremely early. Soon I made the unfortunate discovery that I could sleep right through an alarm clock and not even remember turning it off! My flesh was definitely fighting the priority time with God.

After praying about it, God gave me a humorous but effective solution. I purchased a very loud radio alarm and placed it outside of my room and far down the hall. I would have to quickly rise and walk a distance to turn it off before it disturbed everyone else in the house! I also placed a coffee maker beside the alarm clock and set the coffee timer for five minutes before the alarm sounded. Each morning as I stumbled down the hall to turn off the alarm, there sat the freshly brewed coffee along with my favorite cup. Those early mornings with God soon became some of the best of my entire life!!

Now to some, it may sound silly to go to such lengths to make sure I did not oversleep. But friend, that's just the point! *Whatever it takes to insure and guard your time with God, you must do it.* Otherwise, your flesh will pressure you out of it! You will probably need to take your phone off the hook and tell people that you are not to be disturbed during your primary prayer time. As much as is possible, you should find a place and time to be alone. (Even if you have to go outside and sit in a car.) Your commitment to prayer must be absolute, or you will become inconsistent.

Third Reason for Absolute Commitment - The world's system of human strength and promotion is the direct opposite of God's ways.

The following Scriptures contain a much needed truth for today's program-oriented Christianity. Judges 7:2: "And the Lord said unto Gideon, 'The people that are with thee are too many for me to give the Midianites into their hands, lest Israel vaunt themselves against me, saying, Mine own hand hath saved me.'" Isaiah 55:8: "For my thoughts are not your thoughts, neither are your ways my ways, saith the Lord."

Beyond question, God's ways are *opposite* of man's ways. We tend to place our biggest emphasis and time on human organization, strategies, and methodology. The world's pattern is to develop and exalt human programs, strengths and abilities. Yet, as the Scriptures clearly show, God's pattern is to bring us to a point of utter weakness and total reliance on Himself (2 Corinthians 12:9).

God is displeased when we put the predominate emphasis on our own methods and a comparatively small emphasis on prayer. Yet unfortunately, this is still the typical pattern in much of today's Christianity. We may give casual lip service to prayer, but prayer is definitely not the major practice or priority. Merely, "saying" prayer is vital is not the same as "practicing" it as vital.

Friend, your commitment to develop a powerful prayer life must be absolute because you will not be moving with the crowd. A truly powerful prayer life is simply not the practice of the vast majority of believers (even many Christian leaders and programs). However, I believe a change is in the air. God's people are slowly beginning to return to deeper spiritual cleansing, humility and prayer! Let's now consider the next phrase in the second foundation.

You must make an absolute commitment *to consistently spend significant time* alone with God in uninterrupted prayer.

What does it mean to consistently spend significant time alone with God? I believe the best understanding is a *daily* time with God. Beyond question, that is the strongest biblical pattern. However, it is also important to avoid legalism. Remember, your prayer time must be viewed as a *relationship*, not some duty or rigid requirement. Though it is vital to be disciplined for a regular time with God, you should not feel condemned when there are occasional variations to the pattern. God does not want you to be "fearfully" watching your clock or dreading His condemnation if you fall a few minutes short.

It is also important to understand the meaning of *significant* time with God. Just how much time is significant? Though I would never try to specify a required amount, I can say what is not significant time. **A three or four minute daily devotion is not what is meant by a powerful prayer life.** In such a brief period, there is simply not enough time to develop and experience all the essential types of prayer. Three or four minutes are not enough to fully develop a powerful, well-rounded relationship with God.

I make the general suggestion of spending at least 30 minutes to an hour in a daily prayer time. Though there is nothing magic about the 30 minute minimum, this usually provides enough time to experience most of the basic types of prayer. As we later examine the different types of prayer, it will become clear why a powerful prayer life requires more than a minute or two each day. We now consider the last phrase in the second prayer foundation.

**You must make an absolute commitment
to consistently spend significant time
*alone with God in uninterrupted prayer.***

Why is it foundational to spend time alone in *uninterrupted* prayer? Four reasons seem to be most crucial.

1. Time alone with God is the biblical example of Jesus Christ and the lives of powerful Christians throughout history. Since Jesus is our primary example, this practice is clearly something we should embrace (Luke 6:12; 9:18; Mark 1:33-35).

2. The Scriptures state the importance of a solitary place to seek God's face. Matthew 6:6: "But thou, when thou prayest, enter into thy closet, and when thou has shut thy door, pray to thy Father which is in secret; and thy father which seeth in secret shall hear thee openly."

3. When we pray, we commune with the God of the entire universe and He deserves our undivided attention. Jeremiah 29:13: "And ye shall seek me, and find me, when ye shall search for me with all your heart." How can we even imagine having a serious audience with the God of the universe while distracted by other things? (Since we would never treat an earthly leader with such disregard, why would we thus treat God?)

4. God often speaks in a still, small voice and we must still our hearts to clearly hear His voice. It is impossible to give God our undivided attention while doing something else at the same time.

Beyond question, the development of a truly powerful prayer life requires consistent time alone with God. However, in no way does this suggest that we shouldn't pray throughout the entire day. Indeed, Paul said we are to "pray without ceasing" (1 Thessalonians 5:17). Though it is certainly important to pray while we drive to work or wash the dishes, this can never replace the intense undivided prayer that Jesus called the "closet prayer."

In Luke 11:1, Jesus' disciples made their wisest request when they said, "Lord, teach us to pray." This is perhaps the greatest request any Christian can make of the Father. Yet, concerning prayer we should remember one great truth. *We only learn to pray by praying.* We do not learn to pray primarily by reading books, or attending conferences! (Though these can be very helpful.) To learn to pray, we must consistently show up for "practice." Friend, there is one primary place for practice. That place is your significant daily time alone with the Father! Before we leave this second prayer foundation, I want to share the parable of the "Football Coach."

The Parable of the Football Coach

In our story, a huge high school student walked up to the football coach and told him that he wanted to play football. The coach was thrilled and said, "Son, I'm so glad you want to play. We sure need a player of your size." Then the coach told the young man to be at practice the following day and assured him he would get a chance to play on the team.

For the next three days, the coach anxiously watched for the young man but he never showed up for practice. About a week later, the student again came to the coach and said, "Coach, I sure love football and I really want to be on the team." The coach said, "I'm glad to hear that but you never came to practice. Son, we really need you on our team but if you want to play ball, you must come to practice." The young man assured the coach he would be at practice the next day.

A whole week passed yet, the boy never attended a single practice. Later, the young man saw the coach walking at a distance and he yelled for the coach to wait up so he could talk to him. But rather than stopping, the coach just kept walking. The young man ran to the coach, got right in front of him and started to give him the all too familiar speech. As the boy proclaimed his desire to play, the coach suddenly interrupted him and spoke the following words:

"No son, you really *don't* want to play football. I told you in order to play you must come to practice. The truth is, you had rather do other things than pay the price to be on the team. When you say you want to play, yet you won't come to practice, you are really just kidding yourself. Now excuse me while I go and coach the boys who are waiting at practice. You see son, they *do* want to play football."

The Spiritual Application

Many of us often make the following statement to God, "Lord, I really want to grow spiritually and I want you to use me in your Kingdom. I truly want to know you and see revival in my church and in my nation. Lord, I want you to fill me with the Holy Spirit and teach me to pray in mighty power."

Yet, God immediately says to us, "If you truly want these things, then you must be willing to show up for practice and pay the price in consistent prayer" (Jeremiah 29:13, John 15:5-8). Mark this well — the "place of practice" is spending much personal time with God in daily prayer. Friend, if we say we want to grow and yet we seldom show up for serious prayer, we are just kidding ourselves! God *cannot* teach you to pray if you refuse to show up for practice! Do you now begin to see why this second foundation is so crucial? Until you make the serious commitment to a significant daily prayer time, you can never go on to full maturity in Christ. You will never become powerful in prayer until you give God the daily time to make you one.

At this point, I want to again give you great encouragement and hope. By God's grace, you can do this! If you will begin with just 30 to 45 minutes each day, God will revolutionize your life, family and ministry. In essence, it comes down to a simple daily choice. It's either, "Yes I will spend time with God or, no I will not." Starting right now, I pray your answer will be yes.

Thus far we have examined the first two foundations of a powerful prayer life: first, viewing prayer as a relationship with God and second, spending significant time in daily prayer. We now turn our attention to the third foundation which is absolutely crucial to spiritual growth and power.

Third Foundation of a Powerful Prayer Life:

A powerful prayer life requires the "balanced practice" of all five types of prayer.

A powerful prayer life must be a biblically balanced prayer life. But what do we mean by "biblically balanced?" Perhaps the illustration of a balanced diet will shed light. We all know what is meant by a "balanced diet." In a balanced diet, we regularly eat from all the basic food groups and we eat in the proper amounts. In fact, we all know what happens if you only eat from one or two food groups and completely ignore all the others. It wouldn't take long for you to become sick from malnutrition. Friend, this same principle applies for a balanced prayer life.

In general, there are five basic types of prayer. If you only pray one or two types of prayers and regularly neglect the other three, you *cannot* have a powerful growing relationship with Christ. Your spiritual growth and usefulness will be stunted. Just as an unbalanced diet will cause physical weakness, an unbalanced prayer life will cause spiritual weakness.

It is vital to understand *why* God gave us the different types of prayer. Each type of prayer has a very unique role in developing and maintaining your relationship with Christ. To be weak and inconsistent in any one of the basic prayer types, is to be weak in your relationship and service to God.

In order to understand a balanced prayer life, we must first familiarize ourselves with the different types of prayer. Though we could identify many variations, five categories represent the basic types and each type is essential to developing a particular aspect of your relationship with God. In general, the five prayer types are:

    (1) Praise, thanksgiving and worship
    (2) Confession and repentance

(3) Petition and supplication

(4) Intercession

(5) Meditation (listening prayer and reflection)

If you consistently neglect any of the five types of prayer, your relationship with God will be limited. But do not despair! You can understand and experience all the prayer types in your relationship with God. In the next chapter you will see how.

Questions for
Discussion and Reflection

1. In your own words, explain why it is so important to view prayer as a relationship (Matthew 22:37; John 17:3 and 1 Corinthians 13:1-4).

2. What does it say to God when you choose to make little time for Bible reading and prayer?

3. What is the common denominator in almost every life greatly used by God?

4. Explain the three reasons we must make an absolute commitment to spend significant time alone with God.

5. How would you define a biblically balanced prayer life? Why is a balanced prayer life so important?

Prayers for Daily Growth

* Lord Jesus, help me make our relationship the
greatest priority of my life. Help me not put my
activities or ministries ahead of a love relationship with You. May I never get so busy "for"
You that I neglect time "with" You (Luke 10:38).

* Father, teach me that I can do nothing apart from
You. Fill me with the desire to tarry long in Your
presence. Help me pray and abide close, that
Christ may live His life through me (John 15:1-
8).

* God, grant me such hunger for You that I would
not neglect any of the essential types of prayer
and relationship with You.

Chapter Two

Understanding the Five Basic Types of Prayer

In this chapter, we identify the five basic types of prayer and describe their unique impact on your relationship with God. It is essential to understand and practice *each* prayer type on a regular basis. Each type of prayer has a unique and vital role in the believer's relationship with God. For this reason, no prayer type is more or less important than the others. As you read about the various prayer types, ask God to reveal how your prayer life needs adjustment.

First Type of Prayer: Praise and Thanksgiving - Praise and thanksgiving are the primary ways we give daily adoration and worship to God.

An essential part of relationship with God is the daily (or regular) time of worship and praise. After all, our primary purpose is to praise and worship the Father. And again, what is the supreme commandment in all of Scripture? It is found in Matthew 22:37 "Thou shalt love the Lord thy God with all thy heart, and with all thy soul, and with all thy mind." Clearly this passage calls for a consistent practice of daily praise and thanksgiving.

Yet to many people, prayer consists mostly of bringing a list of needs and wants to God. How sad! We typically blaze through a praise time so we can get to our wish list. In essence, this is the very opposite of God's priority and emphasis. More than anything, God wants your heartfelt praise and worship. And friend, when we get our praise right, God is even quicker to answer prayer! A balanced biblical prayer life absolutely *requires* consistent time in deep praise and thanksgiving to God. We should daily ask God to grow us in effective praise and worship. We must make adequate space in our prayer time to experience genuine praise and thanksgiving.

Scriptures for reference: Psalms 100:1-5, Psalms 50:23, Psalms 22:3; 1 Thessalonians 5:16-18 and Hebrews 13:15

Second Type of Prayer: Confession - Consistent confession is the primary way we receive God's forgiveness and maintain a Spirit-filled life.

It is impossible to maintain a Spirit-empowered life without a consistent pattern of daily confession and repentance! Consistent confession and cleansing represent the primary ways we grow and become conformed to the image of Christ. In fact, according to Psalms 66:18, failure to practice regular confession completely blocks the flow of answered prayer. "If I regard iniquity in my heart, the Lord will not hear me." Thorough confession must be a consistent part of every balanced prayer life.

For confession to be genuine, it must also be *thorough*. The psalmist said, "Search me O God and see if there be any wicked way in me" (Psalms 139:23-24). God's searching clearly implies a "thorough" process. Friend, you couldn't search a cluttered room by a brief, casual glance any more than your heart could be searched by a ten second examination.

Far too many believers ask God to search their heart and then give Him about ten seconds to do it! We often race through a confession time so we can quickly get to our list of wants and needs. A balanced, biblical prayer life *requires* significant time in regular confession to God. Only then can God keep us truly filled and empowered by the Holy Spirit.

Unfortunately, the following statement represents the way Christians often practice confession. "God, is there anything wrong in my life? Is there anything I need to change?" After a quick ten second pause, we then say, "I guess not, now let me give you my prayer list." Now that may sound a bit humorous, but it is sadly descriptive of the practice of millions. Friend, no one could walk in God's fullness with such a shallow practice of confession and cleansing.

Scriptures for reference: 2 Chronicles 7:14, Proverbs 28:13,

Psalms 51:6-10, Psalms 24:3-5, Psalms 66:18, 1 John 1:9, Matthew 5:23 and Matthew 6:14

Third Type of Prayer: Petition - Petition is the type of prayer in which we present our individual needs and desires to God.

Beyond question, God wants us to come to Him with every need and concern. There is certainly nothing selfish about presenting our needs to God. In fact, God invites us to do just that! Jesus' words in John 16:24 reveal the Father's gracious heart toward His children. "Hitherto have you asked nothing in my name: ask, and you shall receive, that your joy may be full." However, it is critical that we learn to focus our personal petitions on God's greatest priorities for our lives.

The more time you spend with the Father, the more you will learn to ask petitions that bring the most eternal good. As you learn to let God guide your petitions, you will see more and more miraculous answers. A balanced prayer life is built on personal petitions that are biblically based and born from the heart of God Himself.

Scriptures for reference: Philippians 4:6-7, Hebrews 4:15-16, John 15:7

Fourth Type of Prayer: Intercession - Intercession is the type of prayer that focuses on the needs of others.

To intercede for someone is to spiritually stand in the gap as mentioned in Ezekiel 22:30, "And I sought for a man among them, that should make up the hedge, and stand in the gap before me for the land, that I should not destroy it: but I found none." The Ezekiel passage describes intercession for a whole nation in rebellion against God. Intercession is also the type used for a backslidden Christian or the salvation of a lost person.

However, intercession is not just for people who are backslidden or lost. It is also vital to intercede for those in significant service to God. (Such as evangelists, missionaries, pastors and teachers.) Praying for those with physical needs represents yet another type of intercession. Intercession is a broad category of prayer that covers anything from praying for the lost to praying for God's blessing on a great evangelist or pastor. God has ordained intercession as the *primary* way He works to save the lost and empower the church.

It is important to note that God has called *all* believers to intercession. Though some are called to far greater levels, no believer can say, "Intercession is not for me." All believers are to practice at least basic levels of intercession on a regular basis (1 Timothy 2:1-2).

Tragically, intercession is the least practiced prayer type because it requires focus outside our own immediate circle. It is also the most crucial type of prayer for reaching the lost and renewing the church. A biblically balanced prayer life must include consistent intercession for all the great Kingdom issues.

Scriptures for reference: 1 Samuel 12:23, Ezekiel 22:30, 2 Timothy 2:1

Fifth Type of Prayer: Meditation - The act of reflecting on God's Word and quietly listening for His still small voice.

To some it may seem odd to include meditation as a type of prayer. I have included it because of my primary definition of prayer. "Prayer is a relationship far more than a mere ritual or discipline." Since prayer is a relationship with God, how can we have a balanced relationship if we do all the talking? A healthy relationship must be two-way! In the prayer time, meditation is the period in which you quietly reflect on your Scripture reading and the impressions God has given. An excellent habit is to write down any impressions or Scriptures God impresses on your spirit. I *strongly* suggest that you keep a daily prayer journal.

Meditation enables us to experience a personal relationship with God as opposed to merely reciting a list of needs and wants. When we pray *we* talk to God; when we mediate *He* talks to us. A biblically balanced prayer life includes time to pause and listen for God's still small voice. (After all, God usually doesn't shout.) He speaks most to those who consistently still their hearts to listen. "You will search for me and you will find me when you search for me with all your heart" (Jeremiah 29:13).

I even go so far as to say that "listening to God" is the fundamental key to an effective prayer life. All genuine prayer starts with God Himself! After all, prayer is not us telling God what He is to do. Prayer is our discovering what God wants to do and joining Him as co-laborers through our prayers. Through meditating, you learn to hear God's leading and thus your prayers initiate from His heart and mind.

Scriptures for reference: Psalms 1:2, 63:6, 77:12, 143:5, 119:15, 119:148; Jeremiah 29:13, 1 John 5:14-15

Why All the Prayer Types are Essential!

Now that we have described the basic types of prayer, it is vital to understand their "inter-connectedness." Each prayer type is designed to develop a particular part of your relationship with God. The consistent practice of each prayer type is absolutely essential to a powerful well-rounded relationship with God. No believer can afford to be weak or inconsistent in *any* of the major types of prayer. Sadly, many people do not view prayer as a rich personal relationship with Christ, but more as a means to secure their own perceived needs or wants.

Unfortunately, the typical pattern is to quickly race through thanksgiving and confession so we can get right to our want lists. And in the lives of far too many, prayer consists of a few personal petitions with little or no intercession for larger Kingdom concerns. Brethren, if we follow such a pattern, we are seriously stunted in spiritual growth and usefulness to God.

To further illustrate the need for balanced prayer, let us again consider the illustration of a balanced diet. Suppose all you ate was one type of food. In fact, what if all you ate was chocolate cake? Well friend, it would not take long for you to become very sick. You would become sick because healthy human beings require a steady diet of all the major food groups. In exactly the same way, God gave us the various types of prayer to develop a rich, healthy relationship with Himself.

If you neglect regular time in adoration, praise and thanksgiving, you are neglecting personal worship which is the first and primary thing God desires. If you neglect regular confession and cleansing, God will not hear your prayers. "If I regard iniquity in my heart, the Lord will not hear me" (Psalms 66:18). When you neglect intercession, you are neglecting a primary command God has given to all believers. You are neglecting God's primary method for drawing the lost and empowering the church.

You must further note that a balanced biblical prayer life does not happen by accident. To really grow in prayer, the believer should understand two things. First, believers must fully realize that all five prayer types need to be a significant part of their daily prayer life. (Many believers do not yet grasp the importance of being consistent in all the prayer types.) Second, believers must make the commitment to seek growth in the various types of prayer. Obviously, this requires a consistent time commitment.

There is no way anyone can experience the five basic prayer types if they only pray four or five minutes a day! Do you now begin to see how the three prayer foundations are interrelated? When you view your prayer time as a relationship and give God significant time, then and only then can He lead you into the full experience of balanced biblical prayer.

Developing a powerful prayer life definitely requires a daily commitment and Spirit-led discipline. If the only time you praise and thank God is when you happen to "feel" like it, then your praise life will be weak and inconsistent. If the only time you practice thorough confession is when you "feel" like it, then you will seldom walk in the fullness of God's Spirit. A balanced, biblical prayer life requires making the daily choice and commitment to allow God to lead you in a full rich relationship with Himself. But believer, do not be discouraged. Your loving

Father is more than ready to help you develop a balanced, biblical prayer life.

About now, some readers may be feeling a bit overwhelmed. After reading this section, a powerful prayer life might seem beyond your reach. Please do not be discouraged! God's grace is more than sufficient and you can develop a powerful prayer life. Our God is so wonderfully patient and gracious. He will take you right where you are and lovingly guide you to ever deeper levels of prayer.

At this point, I must stress what I do not mean by a balanced prayer life. A balanced prayer life is not becoming so regimented and programmed that you always spend exactly the same amount of time in each prayer type. Prayer must not become some legalistic formula that is used in a mechanical manner. *Remember, your prayer life is a personal relationship with a living God.*

As in any relationship, there will be variations in the type of communication needed for each new day. Some days you will be led to spend more time in praise and worship, while other days require much more time in confession. On other days, God will impress you to spend more time in intercession and petition. Your prayer life must be a dynamic, living relationship with God, not some rigid program that never varies.

Though the overall guiding principle is to faithfully spend time in all the different prayer types, you do not have to use the various prayer types in the same order or amount each day. In fact, some days God may lead you to spend almost all your time in only one or two prayer types. Yet, in a general sense, all the prayer types will be a consistent expression of your personal relationship with God.

Conclusion and Summary

God intends for all His children to have a dynamic relationship with Himself. He describes the Church as His bride, and He longs to have a personal, loving relationship with all His children. The very heart of that love relationship is your prayer life!

God further intends for all His children to be powerful in their prayers. No child of God should feel that miraculous answers are beyond reach. If you are saved, you are not only *able* but *responsible* to develop a powerful prayer relationship with Christ. It requires a daily choice!

No doubt we all wish we could make one glorious commitment that would last forever. The truth is, we must all decide to spend daily quality time with God. Certainly the longer we do it, the easier it becomes, but Satan will never stop trying to get us to neglect our prayer time. However, we should always remember one glorious truth, Jesus Christ is Lord and Satan is defeated. By God's grace, you *can* be a powerful intercessor! At this point please prayerfully consider three key questions.

First Question: Have you viewed your prayer time as a personal relationship or as some duty you are required to perform?

If your prayer life is primarily viewed as anything but a love relationship with Christ, then you are missing the whole purpose of prayer, of ministry, and of life itself. "And this is life eternal, that they might know thee the only true God, and Jesus Christ, whom thou hast sent" (John 17:3). Would you now stop and sincerely ask God to help you view your prayer life as a deep personal relationship with Him? Ask Him to forgive you for neglecting your relationship with Him. Claim God's grace for a glorious new relationship with Him.

Second Question: Do you sense God's conviction that your prayer time has been too brief, or inconsistent?

If so, you will now make one of two responses. You will either make a definite commitment to give God more time or you will ignore His leading. Would you now pause and make a genuine commitment concerning the amount of time you spend with God?

Be specific and decide how much time you will commit to God. Decide the specific time and place. Show your seriousness by writing down and sharing your commitment with a friend. Be accountable to someone.

Third Question: Do you sense that you are weak in some of the basic types of prayer?

A full and balanced relationship with Christ *requires* a balanced practice of *all* the various prayer types. Won't you now pause and ask God to help you grow in all of the crucial categories of prayer? Tell God of your commitment to develop a biblically balanced relationship.

In the next chapters, I will outline a practical biblical pattern for developing powerful prayer and a dynamic relationship with Christ. I pray that every reader has now embraced the three foundations of a powerful prayer life. If not, then no guideline will be of much value. But friend, if you are ready to make real time for daily prayer, *nothing* can keep you from an incredible prayer life. Do not be disheartened. With God, all things are possible!

Questions for
Discussion and Reflection

1. Why do you think significant time in daily praise is so vital to prayer and pleasing to God? What does it suggest when we rush through praise to get to our list of needs?

2. Why is significant time in daily confession so essential to spiritual power? What does it suggest when we quickly gloss over confession to get to our prayer lists?

3. Should our petitions center on earthly or eternal concerns? Explain your answer.

4. Why should intercession be a regular part of every believer's prayer life? Give examples of important subjects for consistent intercession.

5. In what way is meditation the "listening" element of your prayer relationship with God? Why is listening such a vital part of genuine prayer?

Prayers for Daily Growth

* Father, please forgive me for viewing my prayer time as a duty or ritual. Help me to treasure my time in prayer because I love and treasure You (1 Corinthians 13:3).

* God, please forgive me for spending so little time with You. Forgive me for being inconsistent in prayer. Help me to make our time together my top priority.

* Lord, please forgive me for neglecting some of the essential types of prayer. Help me walk in a balanced relationship with You.

Chapter Three

*Beginning Guidelines for a
Powerful Prayer Life*

Modern believers frequently ask for a practical pattern or plan to help them pray effectively. Indeed, many Scriptures emphasize the importance of learning to pray effective prayers. Since James 5:16 states that some prayers are *effectual*, we must conclude that some prayers are not effective. In the same spirit, Jesus' disciples made perhaps their wisest request when they said, "Lord teach us to pray" (Luke 11:1).

It is truly sad that many Christians are praying on ineffective levels and don't even realize it. In this chapter, our purpose is to help you embrace simple patterns that will revolutionize your praying. Before I outline a practical prayer pattern, it is important to remember two preliminary principles before you even start.

Two Things to Remember

1. The regular reading of significant amounts of Scripture is absolutely essential to your prayer life.

It is impossible to develop powerful biblical praying without joining your prayers to the promises of God's Word. Romans 10:17 reveals the importance of God's Word to our faith. "Faith comes by hearing and hearing by the Word of God." There can be no powerful prayer life without a growing knowledge of God's truth.

Jesus even stated that we live by every word that proceeds from God (Matthew 4:4). It is also vital to realize you need significant portions of Scripture. You could no more be physically healthy on one or two bites of food than you can be spiritually healthy on occasional tiny bits of Scripture.

In 1 John 5:14-15, we see further evidence of the importance of God's Word in prayer. "And this is the confidence that we have in him, that, if we ask any thing according to his will, he heareth us; And if we know that he hear us, whatsoever we ask, we know that we have the petitions that we desired of him." When we know God's Word, we know His will and then we know how to pray. Furthermore, when we pray in His will, we know the answers are on the way. In order to insure a powerful prayer life, I make two suggestions concerning God's Word.

First: Spend daily time reading and meditating on God's Word. I encourage you to utilize one of today's excellent programs for reading through the entire Bible at least once each year. Most of these schedules involve daily reading from both the Old and New Testaments. In that way you get a balance of Scripture from different parts of the Bible. The important thing is to be consistent and follow God's specific leading for your own time in His Word.

You should also invest in a practical study Bible. The handy references will help you quickly research other Scriptures as you read.

Second: After your Bible reading, write down key insights that God speaks to your heart. In this way you are meditating on God's Word and thus you allow Him to speak directly to your heart. Your Bible reading and prayer then becomes more than just a discipline; you experience a personal love relationship with Christ! As well as your speaking to God, you are giving God the time to speak to you. This practice will revolutionize your relationship with God. Invest in one of today's excellent journaling tools for daily prayer.

2. Familiarize yourself with the basic guidelines and biblical principles for powerful prayer.

Just as there are basic principles for any activity, there are definite patterns for effective prayer. Only when we follow God's rules will His mighty power be released. Tragically, many Christians cannot even name the basic principles of powerful prayer (much less practice them). In the following paragraphs, we identify and describe three guidelines and eight principles of powerful prayer.

Three Practical Guidelines for Powerful Prayer

a.) Be prepared to give God the best time of your day. A significant amount of quality time is vitally important. One hour is a good working goal. Give God your undivided attention. Approach this time as a relationship with God.

b.) Purpose to experience a "balanced" prayer life. Become familiar with the five types of prayer communication and seek to let God guide as you daily move through the various types of prayer.

c.) Daily ask God to teach you to pray (Luke 11:1). Seek a fresh encounter with God and do not fall into the trap of dry routine. Remember, you can only experience genuine prayer by the enablement of the Holy Spirit. Always ask for God's anointing and leading as you pray.

Become Familiar With The Eight Principles of Powerful Prayer

1. **Pray with an attitude of authority and confidence through the name of Jesus.** We are to come in Jesus' name, confident He forgives, knowing He invited us to pray big prayers (John 14:13-14, "And whatsoever ye shall ask in my name, that will I do, that the Father may be glorified in the Son. If ye shall ask any thing in my name, I will do it"), and be assured of His powerful answers (Hebrews 4:16, "Let us therefore come boldly unto the throne of grace, that we may obtain mercy, and find grace to help in time of need").

   Friend, we do not approach God from our own initiative, He invites us! We do not come in our own righteousness, we come in His! Therefore, we are not to approach God with a lack of confidence or hope. When we come in Jesus' name, we are coming in His authority, not our own. You must believe that your prayers have mountain-moving power because you are coming at His invitation, not your own initiative. Don't ever say, "I can't be a powerful intercessor" when God says you can. Remember, your prayers are only as powerful as you think they are.

2. **Spend quality time allowing God to search you so you are freshly cleansed from every sin or hindrance.** (Proverbs 28:13, "He that covereth his sins shall not prosper: but whoso confesseth and forsaketh them shall have mercy.") I suggest that you use a confession guide-sheet or aid. In this manner you can make sure God is hearing your requests. (See pages 83-86 for practical help.) It is vital that your confession and repentance be thorough. Do not rush through your confession time in a brief or casual manner. The book *Returning to Holiness* is designed for the purpose of thorough daily cleansing and growth. (See back of this book for information.)

3. **Specifically ask Him to fill and anoint you with His Spirit** (Ephesians 5:18). Remember, you are about to embark on a ministry that requires the mighty power of the Holy Spirit. Determine to be sensitive to promptings and burdens He gives you as you pray. (Romans 8:26, "Likewise the Spirit also helpeth our infirmities; for we know not what we should pray for as we ought: but the Spirit Himself, maketh intercession for us with groanings which cannot be uttered.") You can no more pray in power without the fullness of God's Spirit than you could physically lift a locomotive.

4. **Determine to pray in genuine faith and expectancy.** (Mark 11:22-24 "And Jesus answering saith unto them, 'Have faith in God. For verily I say unto you, that whosoever shall say unto this mountain, Be thou removed, and be thou cast into the sea; and shall not doubt in his heart, but shall believe that those things which he saith shall come to pass; he shall have whatsoever he saith.'") Ask for promises that directly relate to your prayers. Only believing prayer has power with God. Use God's Word to find the will of God in your praying (1 John 5:14-15, Romans 10:17). It is vital to remember that faith must be a "choice" and more than a mere "feeling." There

will be many times you must choose to believe and keep praying in spite of circumstances and feelings to the contrary.

5. **Ask God to prevent the influence of Satan in yourself and
   in the subjects for which you pray.** Remember, entering a
   serious time of prayer is like being a soldier entering the battle-
   field. Be sure your armor is on! (Ephesians 6:11, "Put on the
   whole armor of God, that ye may be able to stand against the
   wiles of the devil.") Prayer is not just how we prepare for
   spiritual battle, prayer *is* the battle.

6. **Ask God for the spirit of fervency in your praying.** "The
   effectual fervent prayer of a righteous man availeth much"
   (James 5:16). Periodic fasting can be very helpful toward increasing the fervency and power of your prayers. When you
   start to pray, believe God to fill you with His own intense
   passion and love.

7. **In your praying be as specific as possible.** (Philippians 4:6,
   "Be anxious for nothing; but in every thing by prayer and
   supplication with thanksgiving let your requests be made
   known unto God.") General prayers yield little results. Specific prayer moves mountains! Ask God to give you very specific requests that are Scripture-based. It is vital to learn to
   pray the very Word of God.

8. **Concerning your key prayer requests, seek to find committed partners who will agree with you in united prayer.**
   (Matthew 18:19, "Again I say unto you, that if two of you
   shall agree on earth as touching any thing that they shall ask,
   it shall be done for them of my Father which is in heaven.")
   There is special power when believers unite in specific prayers
   of faith. Every great revival and spiritual awakening was born
   from intense, united prayer.

Above all, remember that a powerful prayer life is the only way to
a dynamic, growing relationship with the Father. Genuine prayer
is not a ritual or exercise; it is the very heart of a powerful
relationship with God. In fact, genuine prayer is a relationship!

As you familiarize yourself with the eight prayer principles, God will transform the way you pray. Before you begin your main prayer time, simply take a moment and remind yourself of all the basic principles of powerful prayer. Ask God to help you pray in cooperation with all biblical principles of genuine prayer. The more you adhere to biblical prayer principles, the more the indwelling Christ will pray through you. Miracles will surely follow! In the following chapters, we will examine a practical, biblical pattern for conducting your daily prayer life. And remember, if you will show up for daily practice, God will teach you to pray!

Questions for
Discussion and Reflection

1. According to Matthew 4:4, Romans 10:17 and 1 John 5:14-15, why is Scripture so vital to spiritual health and powerful prayer?

2. Describe two ways to encounter God when you read His Word.

3. In your own words, briefly list and describe the eight principles of powerful prayer.

Prayers for Daily Growth

* Lord Jesus, help me daily meet You in Your Holy Word. Grant that I would no more neglect Your Word than I would neglect to eat my daily meals.

* Father, teach me to pray in the mighty authority and indwelling power of Jesus Christ (John 14:12-14).

* God, grant me the desire to purify my heart before You (1 John 3:3).

* Father, without Your grace I know not how to pray as I ought. Fill me with the Holy Spirit that I may sense Your leading and pray in the ability of Christ Himself (Romans 8:26).

* Lord Jesus, please reveal Your promises and help me pray in genuine mountain-moving faith (Mark 11:22-24, Romans 10:17).

* Father, make me a threshing instrument in prayer. Help me use the weapons of prayer to tear down the strongholds of the enemy (2 Corinthians 10:3-5). Protect me from the wiles and attacks of the enemy.

* God, grant me a fervent heart. Give me eyes that weep over that which makes You weep.

* Lord Jesus, reveal Your words that I may pray according to Your perfect will (Philippians 4:6).

Chapter Four

Phase One:
Approaching God through
Daily Praise and Worship

Is there an exact pattern you must always follow when you come for your prayer time? The quick answer is no. Your daily time with God is a relationship and should always contain an element of *spontaneity and variation*. The goal is to allow the Holy Spirit to direct each time you meet with God. Yet, there are general patterns that are biblical and serve as basic guidelines. In the coming chapters, we will examine an effective biblical pattern by which God leads countless millions in prayer. I will describe the basic elements as "phases" of your daily prayer life.

Phase One: Spend the first several moments in genuine praise, thanksgiving and worship.

In Psalms 100:4, the writer says "Enter His gates with thanksgiving and His courts with praise." In this text, God reminds us to come before Him with a sense of awe, praise, and reverence. We also see this in Jesus' model prayer. "Our Father which art in heaven, hallowed be Thy name" (Luke 11:2). But exactly how do we come to God with genuine praise and worship? I suggest three guidelines.

Steps to a Meaningful Time of Praise

1. Dedicate adequate time to heartfelt praise and worship. Do not try to rush through your time of praise so you can get to your want list! Remember, God wants your heartfelt praise and worship above everything else. A minimum of several minutes should be given to nothing but praise and worship.

2. Spend time thanking God for things He has done in your life. The psalmist says we are to "forget not all His benefits"

(Psalms 103:2). A practical suggestion is to thank God for past, present, and promised future blessings. Ask the Holy Spirit to guide you as you reflect on past, present, and future blessings. Nothing builds your faith and prepares you to pray like thanking God for a significant list of answered prayers!

3.   Spend time praising God for who He is and what He is like (His characteristics). For example, you may praise God because He is: loving, kind, and compassionate; merciful and patient; forgiving and gracious; all powerful and all-knowing; faithful, just; sovereign, King of kings, etc.

I suggest that you pause to meditate on each of God's characteristics and praise Him for what they mean to your life. Don't just "state" His characteristics, take a moment to reflect on what they mean to you now and in the future.

Another pattern for praising God is to meditate on the meaning of His biblical names. Some examples are: (Almighty, Genesis 17:1; Father of Lights, James 1:17; Fortress, 2 Samuel 22:2; I AM, Exodus 3:14; Jehovah (El-Shaddai), Exodus 6:3; Judge, Genesis 18:25; Our Strength, Exodus 15:2; Lord of Lords, Deuteronomy 10:17; Wonderful Counselor, Isaiah 9:6; Our Healer, Jeremiah 17:14; Prince of Peace, Isaiah 9:6; Alpha and Omega, Revelation 1:8; etc.)

When we take time to meditate on who God is and all He has done for us, praise becomes natural and spontaneous. Friend, if you follow these simple biblical suggestions, you will often find yourself spending far more than ten minutes in praise and worship!

Take your time of praise very seriously. One of my daily prayers is that God will increase the depth of my praise and worship. When I began to ask God to help me deepen my worship, I was amazed at the ways He started answering that prayer. When we ask, God continually reveals ways to worship Him in ever- increasing depth.

Believer, when you ask God to teach you to worship, you are

asking something that is very close to His heart. I strongly encourage you to pray for a deeper and purer worship every day of your life. That is a prayer which coincides with God's top priority for His children.

Also learn that you cannot praise only when you "feel" like it. Never forget, the deepest praise and worship is based on a choice, not a feeling. In fact, the deepest worship of your life will be done at times of greatest darkness and pain. At such times you are truly offering God the "sacrifice" of praise. It is only then that the true level of your worship will be seen (Job 1:20,22). After all, anyone can praise God when things are going great.

Like nothing else, praise and worship prepare your heart for dynamic prayer. So often we try to rush into prayer without ever becoming conscious of the majestic glory of the God we address. When we neglect praise, prayer becomes more like a dry ritual than a warm personal relationship. It becomes more like reciting a list, than a two-way conversation with the God of the Universe. The greatest way to secure God's manifest presence is to give Him genuine praise and worship. Remember, "God inhabits the praises of His people" (Psalms 22:3). If you will give regular time to significant praise, God will revolutionize your relationship with Himself!

In the next chapter, I describe a simple process for moving into a time of genuine cleansing and filling with the Holy Spirit. Thorough spiritual cleansing is essential for mountain-moving intercession and petition!

Questions for Discussion and Reflection

1. In your own words, describe at least three steps to a significant time of personal praise and worship.

2. Why do you think some of your deepest worship will occur in times of pain or disappointment?

Prayers for Daily Growth

* Father God, teach me to give you thanks and praise at all times (1 Thessalonians 5:18). Make me keenly aware of the many things for which I should praise, thank and worship you.

* Lord, teach me to worship in ways ever deeper and pure. Enable me to especially worship and praise in times of trial. Teach me to offer the sweet sacrifices of praise (Hebrews 13:15).

Chapter Five

*Phase Two:
Getting Clean Before God
"The Path to Holiness"*

After you have spent time in genuine praise and worship, you are ready to enter a period of confession and cleansing. This is the time God will search your heart and cleanse you from any sin that would hinder your power to pray. It is during the time of confession and repentance that God "corrects" and "adjusts" your life. Confession is how we grow and allow God to conform us to the image of Christ (Romans 8:29; 12:1-2). Holiness and sanctification are two biblical words strangely absent from much modern Christian dialogue. How utterly tragic!

Friend, it is very important that you get fully right with God *before* you start prayers of petition and intercession. James 5:16 reminds us of a crucial truth. "The effective fervent prayer of a righteous man avails much." It is impossible to pray powerful, Spirit-led prayers if there is unconfessed sin between you and God.

The psalmist said, "Search me O God and know my heart: try me, and know my thoughts: And see if there be any wicked way in me and lead me in the way everlasting" (Psalms 139:23-24). God calls for a thorough process and not a brief, casual formality. It is very dangerous for believers to "assume" they are on praying ground. All too often, sin has entered and blocked our power and we are not even aware of it. According to Jeremiah 17:9, it is incredibly easy to ignore and minimize our own sins. "The heart is deceitful above all things, and desperately wicked: who can know it?"

Many people have little prayer power because they fail to practice meaningful confession on a daily basis. Tragically, we tend to rush through our confession time so we can quickly focus on what we want God to do for us. So often, believers say, "Lord, is there anything wrong in my life?" (Then we give God about ten seconds to show us before we move on to our prayer list!) No one can be truly cleansed and full of God's Spirit with such shallow confession!

Because of a lack of confession, many prayers are dry and powerless. We must never forget that God will not hear us if there is unconfessed sin in our life (Psalm 66:18). Mark this well! The depth and power of your prayer life will never be greater than the depth of your daily confession and cleansing. If your confession time is brief, inconsistent and shallow, then so will be your power with God. Please prayerfully consider the following illustration that shows the awesome importance of thorough confession. I think it speaks volumes to today's highly programmed church.

Confession and the Great Shantung Revival

One of the finest examples of thorough confession is the great revival that took place in the Shantung province of China. In the early 1900's, a group of dedicated American missionaries had gone to a tough area of China. It was a hard ministry and the missionaries had sacrificed greatly by even going to such a tough region.

As they faithfully taught and preached God's Word, the Chinese people showed almost no interest and the missionaries redoubled their efforts. They prayed, witnessed and preached as hard as they knew how. They were putting out enormous efforts to love and minister to the Chinese people. Yet, there was very little response and it seemed as if the hearts of the people were made of stone. (Does this sound familiar?)

After many months, the missionaries became disheartened and began to ask God what was wrong. Despite all their hard work and activities, why was there so little spiritual power? God's answer surprised them. In essence He said, "There is hidden unconfessed sin in your life and you are not truly filled with the Holy Spirit." Frankly, it seems incredible to us that such dedicated, hard working missionaries were not filled with the Holy Spirit, yet that is exactly what God told them.

The missionaries agreed to go separately to private prayer places and ask God to show them anything that might be quenching His Spirit. Each missionary took the Bible, a pad and a pen to list their sins. They were then to fully confess and forsake each sin. One of the missionaries was Bertha Smith, who sincerely thought she was close to God and expected to find little to confess. She later stated when she allowed God to search her life, she saw many things she had previously assumed were small and unimportant. Yet, because of the "small" attitudes, she began to realize, she had lost the mighty fullness of the Holy Spirit. These "little" things were huge in the eyes of a thrice Holy God.

Each missionary had the same experience. After a significant time of spiritual searching, the missionaries came together and confessed several things to one another. They then prayed and asked God to fill them with the Holy Spirit. At once, something totally incredible began to happen.

First, God poured out His Spirit on the missionaries! They immediately sensed a joy and power they had never known. The reality of God's manifest presence was overwhelming. There was absolutely no doubt that God had filled and empowered them in a brand new way. Second, their praying and preaching took on awesome new power. Third, God sent a flood of the Holy Spirit upon the entire region. Suddenly, the Chinese people who were so unresponsive, now flooded into the Kingdom of God. Their cold hearts melted before the mighty conviction of God's Spirit. *Frequently the missionaries would be awakened in the middle of the night by people so under conviction they could not wait until morning to be saved!* Many of these missionaries were used to spread revival to countless thousands around the world.

How did God bring this glorious change in the missionaries and such awesome spiritual awakening to the whole region? It happened the same way as every great revival! God's people were genuinely cleansed through deep confession and *then* God filled them with mountain-moving power. Brethren, this is God's changeless pattern for every great revival and spiritual awakening in history. Furthermore, this is the *only* pattern for genuine spiritual fullness and power in your daily life!

Friend, do you grasp the enormous implication of the Shantung revival? If these totally dedicated missionaries were not truly filled with God's Spirit and needed thorough confession, how much more do we? The sad truth is, most believers have gotten so accustomed to living without God's fullness, we have actually forgotten what it is like to be biblically filled with the Holy Spirit. The typical result is we feverishly toil and work for God, yet so little happens. And very often, what does happen doesn't last! We pray and pray, yet few prayers are answered. Why is this? It is because we fail to make serious time to allow God to truly cleanse us and fill us on a daily basis!

So, how much time represents an adequate period of cleansing and repentance? To set some rigid requirement would be legalism. Again, we are talking about a personal relationship and your need for cleansing will naturally vary from day to day. However, you should certainly expect to spend more than a couple of minutes when you ask God to search your life. As a practical rule, I have found it extremely important to examine my life by categories. Rather than trying to search your whole life in one broad sweep, consider each specific category of potential sin. I suggest a daily examination of your life in five basic categories.

Five Categories of Potential Sin

First Category: Sins of Thoughts and Attitudes

Sin begins in the realm of our spirit thoughts and attitudes. Jesus said, "For out of the heart proceeds evil thoughts, murders, adulteries, fornications, thefts, false witness, blasphemies" (Matthew 15:19). In 2 Corinthians 10:5, we are commanded to "take every thought captive to the obedience of Christ." As you examine your thought life, you should ask yourself the following questions: Are there unclean or lustful thoughts, thoughts that are consumed with earthly pursuits, thoughts of anger and bitterness, unloving thoughts, thoughts of fear and doubt, attitudes of pride and prejudice, attitudes of lukewarmness toward God, etc. Pause and reflect carefully after each question. Ask God to reveal any pattern of attitude or thought that is sinful. Immediately confess and forsake these sins of the heart.

Second Category: Sins of Speech

God's Word is clear about the enormous importance of our speech. Matthew 12:36 "But I say unto you, That every idle word that men shall speak, they shall give account thereof in the day of judgement." James 3:10, "Out of the same mouth proceedeth blessing and cursing. My brethren, these things ought not so to be." Even some of the Ten Commandments directly relate to how we use our speech. Deuteronomy 5:11, "Thou shalt not take the name of the Lord thy God in vain."

Some potential sins of speech are as follows: Using course or profane words, gossip, slander, unkind or unloving words to or about others, speech that is overly critical, speaking words that are exaggerations or untruths, speaking when we should be quiet, etc. Be specific in confessing your sins of speech. Be sensitive to the fact that God will lead you to apologize to people you have hurt with your words.

Third Category: Relationship Sins

Perhaps the most common place we lose God's fullness is in our relationships. Relationship sins generally fall in five major areas. In each area, you must be willing to take specific actions of repentance. But by God's mighty grace, you can!

(1) Can you think of people you may have hurt or offended in some manner?

In Matthew 5:23-24, Jesus was emphatic about the importance of getting right with those you have offended. "Therefore, if you bring your gift to the altar, and there remember that your brother has something against you, leave your gift before the altar, and go your way. First be reconciled to your brother, and then come and offer your gift."

In other words, Christ was saying, "Don't approach God until you first get right with those you have offended!" Friend, I am not suggesting this is easy, but Christ clearly says it is absolutely necessary. Many Christians lack power because they have ignored this foundational command.

Take the next several moments to consider those you may have offended. When God reveals people you have hurt or slighted, resolve to go to them and ask their forgiveness. Yet, do not go and try to defend yourself or get the battle started again. Just go in simple humility and love. Furthermore, do not think you have failed if they refuse to forgive you. Your responsibility is to do your part in a humble and loving manner. How they respond is their responsibility.

Tremendous miracles occur in families when someone is humbly willing to ask forgiveness for a wrong. Powerful churchwide revivals have often hinged on one or two church members getting truly right with one another. We must understand that so-called "little" rifts between Christians can easily quench God's Spirit for the whole church! Friend, the Holy Spirit is very sensitive and you must take your relationships seriously.

(2) Are you bitter or holding grudges against people who have offended you?

In Matthew 6:14-15, Jesus made a statement of enormous importance. "For if you forgive men their trespasses, your heavenly Father will also forgive you. But if you do not forgive men their trespasses, neither will your Father forgive your trespasses."

Many a prayer gets no higher than the ceiling because you are holding inner resentment and bitterness against another person. In fact, Jesus says we must forgive people "from the heart." Matthew 18:35, "So my heavenly Father also will do to you, if each of you from his heart, does not forgive his brother his trespasses." It is common for people to "say" they have forgiven someone when in their heart, they really haven't.

Many people hold secret bitterness against friends or family members. In other cases, it may be toward strangers who have wronged you. Especially today, believers need to be aware that we can develop bitterness toward godless politicians, social activists, and entertainers who attack our values. No doubt, we must always stand strong for truth, but we must never harbor hatred against those who attack us. We must never cease to hate sin, but we must always love the sinner. Ask God to search your heart and reveal any patterns of bitterness or unforgiveness.

It is also possible to hold secret bitterness against God. Some people privately resent the fact that God allowed some personal tragedy or didn't answer an urgent prayer. Others harbor bitterness because God blesses others in ways He has not blessed them. Far too many Christians have cooled off in their service and worship because they are hurt or disappointed.

Questions for Reflection: Is there anyone or any situation about which you harbor the slightest bitterness or resentment? Have you secretly resented God for allowing some painful situation in your life? Have you "cooled off" toward God because He disappointed you in some manner? Be honest with yourself and fully confess these sins. Make a definite decision to harbor no bitterness against anyone. And remember, forgiveness is a *choice*, not a *feeling*.

(3) Are you involved in any improper relationships?

An improper relationship could be anything from adultery and fornication to simply being inappropriately close to someone. For example, a young person may be emotionally involved with someone too old or vice versa. A husband may be too emotionally close to a female friend or work mate. A wife may be too emotionally involved with a male friend or work mate. Husbands and wives may be sharing things with others that should only be shared with their mate. Spouses may spend too much time with friends to the neglect of their marriage partner. Parents can be too involved in the lives of their married children or married children too dependent on parents.

You may be involved with someone and while you say "we're just friends," you know it has become more than friendship. Don't try to rationalize or defend a relationship you know is improper. It inevitably opens the door to Satan and leads you into ever-deepening bondage.

Improper relationships involve many things *besides* physical immorality. Because it's so easy to rationalize, this sin has become prevalent among Christians. It is the soil from which adultery and fornication so often grow. Ask God to reveal any relationships that are improper or out of balance. It is vital that you stop it now before it gets worse. Be honest with God and with yourself. And, do not despair, God will give you the strength to change!

(4) Do you neglect regular fellowship and meaningful service through your church?

According to Hebrews 10:25, it is a major sin to neglect regular fellowship and worship with the body of Christ. "Not forsaking the assembling of ourselves together, as is the manner of some, but exhorting one another, and so much the more, as you see the day approaching."

God strongly emphasizes the importance of staying closely connected to a local body of believers. According to 1 Corinthians 12 - 14, all believers are to stay in genuine fellowship and close relationship with a local congregation.

God does not intend for anyone to be a "lone ranger" or an "isolationist"! In our day of selfish individualism, many people like to join a large church so they can get lost in the crowd. They come and receive blessings, but then go home without any real fellowship or closeness with other believers. (And that's exactly the way they want it!) Such a pattern is totally unbiblical and inherently selfish.

Still others seek a church that will "bless them" without asking how they can serve or give in return. Many people selfishly shop for a church like they shop for a health club. They want one with the most benefits and least cost! Churches in growing areas usually have people running out their ears while churches in tough areas (where ministry is so needed) often starve for Christian workers.

Today it seems many want to sit and be served but few want to get up and serve. In seeking a church, our primary prayer should not be "What can this church do for me, but what can I do for this church?" *It is a major sin not to be involved in consistent giving and service through a local body of believers.* Obviously, this principle does not apply to the homebound or seriously ill. Also there are exceptions in the case of those called to itinerant ministries. (Yet, even they need a definite home church!)

Another common form of this sin is the tendency to drift from church to church. Such people often become permanent visitors. By doing this, these believers never form deep biblical fellowship with other Christians. They also avoid personal responsibility and spiritual service for the good of Christ's Church. As a result, they can never grow up spiritually or be truly right with God. Unfortunately, Satan often deceives such people into believing they are somehow fulfilling their responsibility to Christ's body. Ask God to search your life and reveal ways you are neglecting consistent fellowship and substantial service in the local body of Christ.

Questions for Reflection: Are you a spectator rather than a participant in God's work? Do you consistently receive but seldom give? Have you become a permanent visitor who never seems to plug in and serve God? Friend, if you want to be right with God, you must decide to embrace a church and go to work! Resolve now to immediately obey God in full commitment to a local body of believers.

(5) Are your family relationships consistent with God's Word?

Improper family and church relationships are common places we lose the filling and power of God's Spirit. "No one who is wrong with others can be truly right with God." The following Scriptures reveal God's plumb line for husbands, wives and children.

God's special words to husbands and fathers -Ephesians 5:23 - "For the husband is the head of the wife, even as Christ is the head of the church."

From this verse we see that God calls the husband to be the spiritual head of the home. He is responsible to give spiritual guidance and nurture. Every husband and father has a very special responsibility to God and to his family.

Ephesians 5:25 - "Husbands, love your wives, even as Christ also loved the church and gave Himself for it."

The husband is commanded to love his wife with a powerful, sacrificial love. He is to literally sacrifice himself to meet the needs of his wife. The husband is to "give himself" to meet the physical, emotional and spiritual needs of his wife. In every way, he is to place the needs and welfare of his wife ahead of his own.

1 Peter 3:7 - "Likewise, you husbands, dwell with them according to knowledge, giving honor unto the weaker vessel."

The husband is commanded to be very caring and sensitive to his wife's needs. A husband's uncaring, insensitive attitude toward his wife will inevitably hinder his ability to pray (1 Peter 3:7). A godly husband will literally study the unique needs and desires of his wife. This includes physical, emotional, mental, financial and spiritual needs.

Ephesians 6:4 - "And you fathers, provoke not your children to wrath: but bring them up in the nurture and admonition of the Lord."

The father is commanded to relate to his children in loving spiritual guidance, not in anger or wrath. Discipline must done with consistency and love. The father's great priority is the spiritual nurture and training of his family. It is certainly important, but financial provision is by no means the father's primary responsibility.

Questions for Reflection: Husband, have you taken responsibility to lead your family in devotions and prayer? Do you set a loving atmosphere of spiritual nurture and training? Do you put your wife's needs and desires ahead of your own? Do you study to understand and meet the unique emotional needs of your wife? Have you made use of today's excellent books and videos on marriage? Are you providing wise financial guidance and stewardship for the security of your family? Are you guiding your children in spiritual growth and training? Do you discipline your children with consistency and love? Do you consistently talk to your children about spiritual values? A brief daily devotion alone can never replace the value of consistent "talking" with your children in everyday life issues.

Let no husband despair! If you honestly confess your failures, God will give you the powerful grace to change. Today, there are many good books and resources to help you. Don't be overwhelmed. Even though you may feel inept, God will bless even small steps toward fulfilling your spiritual responsibility. Husband, you can see a miracle in your family!

God's special words to wives - Ephesians 5:24, 33 - "Therefore as the church is subject to Christ, so let the wives be to their own husbands in everything...and the wife see that she reverence her husband."

The submission of the wife does not mean the husband can be a harsh master or boss over her. They are equal partners in the grace of Christ. Rather, her submission is the loving and willing submission seen with Christ and His Church. Thus, a godly wife exhibits a beautiful spirit of humility, love and honor toward her husband. She is to have a "gentle and quiet" spirit.

1 Peter 3:3 - "Whose adorning let it not be that outward adorning of plaiting the hair, and of wearing of gold, or of putting on of apparel, but let it be the hidden man of the heart, in that which is not corruptible, even the ornament of a meek and quiet spirit,

which is in the sight of God of great price."

Questions for Reflection: Wives, do you ever treat your husband with dishonor and disrespect? Do you often point out his weaknesses and faults? Do you patiently forgive and treat him kindly in spite of his shortcomings? Do you ignore his needs and desires? Have you grown careless with your health and appearance? Do you have a rebellious spirit toward him? Have you done all you can do to bring your attitude in line with the pattern God has set for you in Scripture? Is your attitude one of thanksgiving and love or complaining and anger?

The greatest way to see God change your husband is to bring yourself under God's pattern for a godly wife. Wives, don't give up on your husband or yourself. Don't make excuses by saying, "I just don't have a gentle and quiet personality." If you honestly surrender to God's pattern, you will see a miracle in your home!

God's special words to parents - Matthew 18:6 - "But whoso shall offend one of these little ones which believe in Me, it were better for him that a millstone were hanged about his neck, and that he were drowned in the depth of the sea."

Because children are incredibly perceptive, they usually pick up more from what parents do than what they say. Often without even realizing it, parents are modeling values and habits that have tragic effects on their children's development. Training up a child in the way he should go is more about daily example than occasionally sharing religious words.

Questions for Reflection: Parents, do you model excitement and joy about worshiping God? Do you consistently express love for Christ's church or a negative complaining attitude? If your children are expressing a negative attitude toward God and His church, you may need to take a serious look at the attitudes you actually model before them.

Parents, do you lovingly and consistently communicate with each other? Do you consistently take time to talk to your children? Do you really listen when your children talk to you? Do you respond with love and understanding or quickly become angry? If your children are pulling away from you, ask God to reveal ways you may have caused it.

Parents, do you model moral purity by the things you talk about? Have you demonstrated holiness by the things you watch or read? Have you consistently communicated God's standards concerning sex and marriage to your children? Do you communicate in a way that reveals understanding about their temptations and struggles? Have you been approachable and loving? If your children are moving towards immorality, ask God if there are ways you should examine your example. If they won't talk to you, ask God if you've contributed to the barrier.

Parents, do you consistently model honesty and respect for others? Do you break speed laws or cheat on taxes? Have you demonstrated the ability to readily admit your own sins and failures? Do you readily admit your sins or do you make excuses? If your children are demonstrating tendencies toward cheating or lying, you should seriously examine your own example.

Parents, by no means do I suggest that children's problems are automatically a result of parental failure. In fact, Satan often heaps false guilt on parents. However, parents face the awesome power of example. May God give parents honesty to fully confess ways that the children have been harmed by attitude and example.

In many cases, parents will need to ask forgiveness of their children (even older or adult children). Such loving honesty will have an enormous healing effect on strained parent-child relationships. Some of the above questions were drawn by permission from "A Christian Parent's Checklist" by Shelia Jones (email address SJonesAZ@aol.com)

God's special words to children and youth - Ephesians 6:1-3: "Children, obey your parents in the Lord: for this is right. Honor your father and mother; which is the first commandment with promise; that it may be well with you and that you may live long on the earth."

Old Testament law pronounced severe punishment on children who cursed or dishonored a parent. Modern children must relearn the extreme importance of honoring their parents. Today's foolish and wicked society has completely reversed the principle of honoring one's parents.

Questions for Reflection: Children or teenagers, do you disobey your parents? Do you often ignore their guidance? Have you treated your parents with disrespect or anger? Disrespect toward parents is a very serious sin before God. Young people, you cannot be right with God if you consistently disrespect your parents.

As adults, we too must ask whether we are honoring our elderly parents. Do you neglect to call and visit your aged parents? Do you neglect your Mother and Father by failing to give them consistent time and attention? Are you neglecting them emotionally or financially? Do you fail to help them with needs around their home? Are there unresolved harsh words or feelings between you and your parents? Have you truly sought to make it right? Remember, no one who mistreats or neglects a parent can be fully right with God!

Fourth Category: Sins of Commission and Transgression

In a broad sense, these are the sins of *doing* something wrong or *breaking* God's laws. Examples of such sins are: adultery, fornication, stealing or dishonesty, assaulting someone, going to sinful places, watching adult rated movies, destructive habits (such as smoking, drinking, overeating or eating unhealthy foods), reading unclean literature, putting recreation or material things ahead of God, idolatry, financial dishonesty, cheating employers, etc.

If you will be honest with God, He will reveal things that He wants to change. Ask God to reveal anything in your life that may be offensive to Him and don't be afraid to own up to your sins. God's grace will cover them all! (1 John 1:9, "If we confess our sins, He is faithful and just to forgive us our sins and cleanse us from all unrighteousness.")

Fifth Category: Sins of Omission

Sins of omission are the failure to obey Christ's commands or conform our character to His image. This sin is mentioned in James 4:17 "Therefore to him that knoweth to do good, and doeth it not, to him it is sin." Some examples of sins of omission are: neglecting Bible reading and prayer, failing to witness, failure to tithe, neglecting regular worship, refusing to use your spiritual gifts in a local church, etc.

When you confess a sin of omission, be sure to take concrete steps to correct it. Confession is not genuine until you make the commitment to forsake the sin. (Proverbs 28:13, "He that covereth his sins shall not prosper: but whosoever confesseth and forsaketh them shall have mercy.")

The five categories of confession in this chapter are quite brief and general. As a companion to this book, I strongly suggest the resource *Returning to Holiness: "A Personal and Churchwide Journey to Revival." Returning to Holiness* takes the reader through a very thorough cleansing journey with God. It is completely Bible-centered and helps believers experience deep repentance and full victory over sin. (For information contact Dr. Frizzell at the address in the front of this book.)

A Final Word About Confession

I can imagine that some readers may be a bit overwhelmed about confession. You may be thinking, "If I have to go through all this every time I pray, I don't have a chance!" Dear friend, please don't be discouraged. I am not suggesting you must meticulously go through *all* of these sin categories every time you pray, but you should at least be aware of key categories and Scriptures. You may simply want to ask God if there is sin in each category and then quietly reflect for a few moments. If nothing is revealed, then move on to the next category. Some days you may be led to focus only on one or two categories. Above all, seek to be spontaneous and sensitive to God's Spirit. Remember, this is a personal *relationship* with God, not a formula!

I do warn you of one potential danger. Be careful to avoid confession that does not lead to immediate repentance. When you become aware of a sin, be sure to take action to remove it. At times, you may need the counsel of a pastor or a prayer partner to help you overcome it. True confession must involve repentance, or it is not genuine! Sin must be confessed and *forsaken* (Proverbs 28:13).

The daily time of confession is God's primary way of conforming you to the image of Christ. It is in this time that God corrects and transforms you in spiritual growth. Scripture-based confession and repentance are God's primary method for transforming you by the renewing of your mind (Romans 12:1-2; 2 Timothy 3:16). God's top priority in the life of every believer is to make him holy and sanctified in body, soul, and spirit (Romans 8:29). Since that is His top priority and the key to your growth, then how could you think you can neglect regular confession and cleansing?

By now I am sure you see even more why you must spend significant time in regular prayer. *No one is going to develop a powerful balanced prayer life in a two or three minute prayer time!* And no one can stay truly cleansed and full of God's Spirit without consistent time in thorough confession. Yes, it does involve a commitment of time and focus. But believer, you *can* do it and the results will be worth it a million times over! In the next chapter you will discover how to pray powerful prayers of personal petition.

Questions for
Discussion and Reflection

1. How do you think God "corrects" and "adjusts" us during times of confession and cleansing?

2. Why is it dangerous for believers to just "assume" they are clean without frequent times of examination? (Jeremiah 17:9).

3. If the dedicated missionaries to Shantung, China needed a deep cleansing and filling, what implication does this have for us?

4. What happens if we try to rush through our time of cleansing?

5. List and briefly describe the five categories of potential sins. Why do you think it is important to use a thorough biblical cleansing guide?

Prayers for Daily Growth

* Father, open my eyes to my sin that I may be fully conformed to the image of Christ (Romans 8:29). Lord, correct me that I may walk in the full freedom of Christ (John 8:34; Romans 6:6,14).

* Wash me O God, that I may be clean and pure. Refine my heart in the beauty of holiness (Psalms 51:7, Proverbs 17:3).

* God, help me be thorough in letting You "search" all categories of my life. Create in me a burning hunger for righteousness (Matthew 5:6). Cause me to pursue holiness through the Christ who lives within my heart (Hebrews 12:14).

Chapter Six

Phase Three:
How to Pray Dynamic Prayers of Petition

We now come to the type of prayer that comes the easiest for most. The "prayer of petition" is how you bring your list of needs and wants to God. I want to state that there is definitely nothing wrong or selfish about bringing your desires and needs to God. Our Father longs to give His children the desires of their heart. (Psalms 37:4, "Delight thyself also in the Lord; and He shall give thee the desires of thine heart.") Indeed, our God is a kind and gracious Father who loves to give good things to His own. (Matthew 7:11, "If ye then, being evil, know how to give good gifts unto your children, how much more shall your Father which is in heaven give good things to them that ask Him?")

In fact, a major sign of intimacy with God is your freedom to tell Him every desire and need of your heart. If you have a close relationship, you are able to talk to God as you would your dearest friend. (After all, He is your dearest friend.) Honest sharing expresses a closeness and dependency that is very pleasing to God.

However, there are crucial points to remember about prayers of petition. Modern believers desperately need to learn how to pray petitions that are biblically based and centered on God's will. In deed, that is our primary objective in this chapter.

So, what type of petitions should make up your personal prayer life? With many believers, petitions focus mostly on personal needs. Some common examples are: physical problems, general emotional needs, personal desires, financial or job concerns, school needs, relationship problems, etc. Indeed it is perfectly appropriate to bring all these concerns to God. However, every believer needs to mature to the point where personal petitions also reflect the top priorities of God. We desperately need to understand the difference between prayer requests that are temporal and those that are eternal and Kingdom-oriented.

Temporal requests primarily relate to earthly needs and concerns. Some examples are: a better job, a new car, a physical healing, etc. Obviously such requests are important and have a legitimate place in our prayer life. *However, "Kingdom requests" are those which focus on issues that are eternal.* Some examples are: your personal growth in the fruit of the Holy Spirit, overcoming a temptation, tearing down a spiritual stronghold, increasing your ministry, leading people to Christ, revival in your church, city or nation, etc. Obviously, God's heart is far more focused on issues that are eternal in nature.

Since God's priorities are on the eternal, shouldn't our personal petitions reflect this same priority? Yet, if modern believers are honest, the vast majority of petitions involve physical and temporal needs. Unfortunately, that is the exact opposite of the pattern God desires for the petitions of His children. *Developing a balanced prayer life means allowing God to "reorder" and "broaden" your personal petitions to reflect Kingdom priorities.* In the paragraphs below, we will examine a practical approach to effective personal petitions.

Three Steps to Powerful Prayers of Petition

1. Regularly pray through each fruit of the Holy Spirit and ask God to develop the image and holiness of Christ within you.

Never forget that God's top priority for your life is the development of Christ's character and holiness in your life (Romans 8:29). Therefore, your personal petitions should relate to the development of His image in your life. But what is the image of Christ and what does He look like in a person's life? I believe Galatians 5:22-23 contains one of the most concise and perfect picture in all of Scripture. "The fruit of the Spirit is love, joy, peace, longsuffering, gentleness, goodness, faith, meekness, temperance."

You could not possibly pray more in the will of God than to pray each spiritual fruit for your life daily. As you pray one by one through the fruit of the Holy Spirit, you are praying for the exact image of Christ to be formed in your life. In 1981, God led me to begin daily praying through all nine fruit of the Spirit. To this day, I have never found anything that comes close to the power of daily praying these character words for my own spiritual growth.

Many believers pray in far too general terms. We pray things like "Lord, just help me be a better Christian" or, "Lord, help me grow and do better." But what do such requests really mean? They are so general they have little focus and thus very little power. On the other hand, the fruit of the Holy Spirit are very specific and provide biblical petitions for powerful spiritual growth.

As you pray through each of the spiritual fruit, you will discover this process also becomes an opportunity for God to search and cleanse your life. With each fruit you not only ask God to fill you with that trait, but you also ask God to reveal how you are not living that particular fruit. The following illustration shows you how to begin with the fruit of love.

Examples of How to Daily Pray the Fruit of the Spirit

Prayers for Love: Father I ask You to fill me with a deep love for You (Romans 5:5). Grant that my love for You be passionate and not lukewarm (Revelation 3:15). Please fill me with Your powerful love for things that further Your Kingdom (Matthew 6:33). Endue me with a love for souls and a passion to grow our church. Fill me with a burning love for serving You. Baptize me with a selfless, compassionate love for my family and for those I meet each day. God, by the power of Your Spirit, please fill my heart with Your powerful love.

Do you believe God would answer the prayers I just described? Of course He would! And why would He answer such prayers? He will answer because you are praying His Word and you are praying in the absolute center of His will! Specific biblical prayer petitions are infinitely more powerful than general requests such as, "Lord, just help me be a better Christian."

Another great advantage of praying the fruit of the Holy Spirit is the fact that God uses such character words to immediately convict and correct His children. Typically as I pray through each fruit, I will pause and ask God to show me how I am not living up to that character word.

Again let's use the word "love" for an example.

Lord, where am I failing to love You with all my heart, soul, mind and strength? How have I put things ahead of You in my time, my thoughts, or my energies? Do my prayers, my service or my worship represent a passionate love or a lukewarm attitude? Lord, how have I failed to have a love and passion for lost souls? Have I expressed love toward my family or have I been unloving? How do I need to change?

Do you begin to see how God can use the fruit of the Holy Spirit to guide your personal petitions and your personal cleansing? Dear reader, I want to make a guarantee. If you ask God to search you at the point of each fruit, you will hear His voice and God will perform a deep cleansing work in your life! This kind of praying is the very essence of discipleship and spiritual growth. This type of prayer is the very heart of pursuing God's holiness (Hebrews 12:14).

In the above illustration, I have shown how you can pray for God's love to flood your life. We have also seen how God can use that one word to search your life. In exactly the same way, each of the fruit should be used as a powerful guide in praying for your own spiritual growth. Absolutely nothing has impacted my life like this one simple practice!

I want to definitely state that you are not required to pray through all nine fruit each day. Though that is certainly possible, you may want to focus on only one or two fruit each day. The exact pattern will vary. *The important thing is that you bring your personal petitions to a greater focus on personal holiness as opposed to only praying for temporal needs.*

As you pray through each fruit, God not only answers, but He cleanses and corrects as you briefly pause to consider each characteristic. Listed below are brief examples for the other eight spiritual fruit.

Sample Prayers for Each Fruit

Joy - Lord, I believe You to fill me with a supernatural joy that is unspeakable and full of glory (1 Peter 1:8). Show me how I fail to rejoice and give praise at all times (Philippians 4:4).

Peace - Lord, I trust You to fill me with Your perfect peace that passes understanding and guards my heart and mind (Philippians 4:6-8). Show me how am I choosing to worry and fret instead of trusting You?

Longsuffering - Lord, I believe You to fill me with the powerful ability to wait on You and calmly endure hardships. In what way am I impatient or complaining?

Gentleness - Lord, I trust You to fill me with kind and gracious attitude toward others. Show me how I have been harsh or unkind to others.

Goodness - Lord, I believe You to fill me with a generous attitude that is always looking to help others. Please show me how I have been selfish and oblivious to the needs of others.

Faith - Lord, I trust You to fill me with powerful mountain-moving faith. Fill me with steadfastness. Lord, show me how I have doubted You.

Meekness - Lord, please fill me with genuine humility, brokenness and a repentant, obedient spirit. Show me how I have been proud, arrogant or rebellious.

Temperance - Lord, please fill me with self-control and discipline. Please show me how I have been undisciplined, careless, or indulgent in any area of my life.

2. Regularly pray through the Beatitudes and ask God to conform you to these godly characteristics (Matthew 5:1-10).

I suggest that you study each of the eight character traits outlined in Christ's Beatitudes. With each beatitude you can follow the same prayer pattern that was outlined for the fruit of the Spirit. Each character trait becomes both a specific prayer and point of personal examination for your life. When you pray for Christ to fill you with these traits, you can again have the assurance that you are praying dead center of His will for your life.

Praying in the center of God's will gives incredible confidence because of the promise of 1 John 5:14-15 "And this is the confidence that we have in Him, that, if we ask any thing according to His will, He heareth us; And if we know that He hear us, whatsoever we ask, we know that we have the petitions that we desired of Him." You cannot go wrong praying the Word of God for your own life! Again I stress that you may not be led to pray through all Beatitudes on a daily basis. Allow God to led you in your unique pattern of prayer.

3. Regularly pray through other character words that are found in Scripture. (Those besides the fruit of the Spirit and the Beatitudes.)

As God has led me in personal prayer, He has given me several biblical character words around which I daily focus my prayers and reflection. Examples of key words are as follows: a) the anointing, power and filling of the Holy Spirit, b) genuine humility and brokenness, c) spiritual zeal and diligence, d) wisdom and discernment, e) immovability, f) steadfastness, g) spiritual soberness, h) a spiritual passion and fervency, i) a spirit of genuine worship, j) purity of motives, k) a quickened mind, l) a spirit of revelation and understanding, m) boldness and spiritual authority, n) spiritual protection from sin, self, Satan, and the world.

When you read Scripture and spend significant time with God, He will reveal several biblical character words to use in your personal prayer petitions. Again, this should not become just a rote, mechanical list. If you are sensitive to God's Spirit, He will guide you as you adjust your focus from day to day.

A Final Word About Petition

Modern Christians desperately need to grow up in their prayer petitions. Far too many are praying personal prayers that are mostly temporal and have little to do with eternal issues. We often treat God more like a Christmas wish catalogue than the sovereign God who desires above all to conform us to the image of Christ! Remember, your true spiritual growth and service will not exceed the depth of your personal petitions. If your personal petitions are brief, non-specific, and temporal, your spiritual growth will be greatly limited.

Most believers are praying petitions that are much too general. We must never forget the importance of *specific* prayers. Until prayers become biblical and specific, they have little power with God. My friend, if you will allow God to make your petitions specific and in line with His will, you will experience growth like you cannot imagine (1 John 5:14-15).

At this point I want to strongly encourage every reader. *Do not be discouraged or overwhelmed by what you have read.* God will guide you into mature praying and the Holy Spirit is an excellent teacher. All you have to do is familiarize yourself with these basic prayer principles and give God significant time in daily prayer. He will do the rest! I trust it is becoming increasingly clear that you can never experience the depths of Christ if all you pray is two or three minutes a day. In the next chapter, you will discover how any believer can become a powerful intercessor!

Questions for
Discussion and Reflection

1. In your own words, describe the difference between temporal and Kingdom-oriented prayer petitions.

2. Why do you think Kingdom-oriented petitions have greater impact than temporal petitions?

3. In what way would praying through the fruit of the Holy Spirit conform you to the image of Christ?

4. Why is praying character words far more important than merely praying for earthly needs and comforts?

Prayers for Daily Growth

* Father, cause me to pray according to Your priority of holiness and sanctification in my daily life. Cleanse and transform me by the washing of the water by the Word (Ephesians 5:26).

* God, instill the spiritual fruit and the Beatitudes into the very fabric of my heart. Reveal many Scriptures to claim for personal holiness and transformation. Help me hide Your words in my heart that I may not sin against You.

Chapter Seven

Phase Four:
Powerful Intercession

We now come to the most powerful yet least practiced of the basic types of prayer. Intercession is the type of prayer that is primarily focused on *the needs of others.* As with petition, we should put a greater priority on interceding for eternal issues as opposed to the temporal. (Though of course, we will do both.)

An excellent description of intercession is found in Ezekiel 22:30 "And I sought for a man among them, that should make up the hedge, and stand in the gap before Me for the land, that I should not destroy it: but I found none." In this text, the intercessor "stands between" God and those who deserve judgement. The prayers of intercessors are God's foundational strategy for evangelism, missions, discipleship, revival, and spiritual awakening. Yet tragically, most denominations and churches put great emphasis on programs, promotions, and strategies while skimping on prayer. The lack of power in many ministries is explained by a very shallow level of intercession.

However, God is beginning to do a great work among His people! More and more churches and individuals are taking intercession seriously. In those people and churches, God's power is beginning to be released in phenomenal ways.

As more and more Christians become interested in intercession, we face an urgent need to teach them how to intercede biblically. Indeed, many are hindered from intercession because they simply do not know how! As with petition prayers, many believers are caught in a type of intercession that is far too general and unfocused. It is time for our intercession to get beyond prayers such as; "Lord, save all the lost people." or "Lord just bless our church." Though such prayers are not technically wrong, they are extremely general and lack the power of specific, biblical intercession. In the next section, I will address two key questions about effective intercession.

Where Do I Focus My Intercession?

When considering subjects for intercession, I suggest you again remember one foundational principle. *Let your greatest focus be issues with eternal rather than temporal significance.*

Though you will certainly intercede about physical and temporal needs, these should not predominate your intercession. The following list represents some of the most important subjects for which all believers should pray regularly.

Key Subjects for Consistent Intercession

1) Spiritual and physical needs of family and friends
2) Spiritual needs of work mates, classmates, and those we see in daily life (gas attendants, waitresses, sales clerks, doctors, etc.)
3) Those who don't know Christ
4) Spiritual growth and protection for new Christians
5) Backslidden believers
6) Your pastor, staff and key lay leaders
7) Revival and growth in your church
8) Missionaries and persecuted believers
9) Key denominational leaders and agencies (local, state, and denominational)
10) Spiritual leaders and key churches of all denominations
11) National leaders (the president, governors, mayors, etc.)
12) Local, state, and national government
13) Sweeping revival and spiritual awakening (local, national and worldwide)
14) Key mission initiatives and strategies (local, state national and global)
15) Key evangelism initiatives and strategies (local, state, national and global)

The fifteen subjects for intercession provide a general prayer guide for every believer. Again, I am not suggesting you must pray through all of these every day. I suggest that you set a pattern in which you pray for certain categories on certain days. As you learn to be sensitive to God's Spirit, you will also sense Him leading you to shift your focus on certain issues from day to day so as to avoid a rigid ritual. The important point is that you broaden your intercession to involve all essential categories and that you remain sensitive to Christ's leading in your daily prayer time.

How Do I Pray "Specific" Prayers of Intercession?

The more specific and biblical our prayers, the more power we have before God. The following sections provide examples of specific intercession for some of the basic categories. Ask Christ to enable you to pray these prayers in the unique manner and wording He gives you.

Examples of Specific Intercessory Prayers

For the lost and backslidden

Lord, pour out Your Spirit upon (name of person) and:
- *Convict* him of his sin and separation from You. John 16:8
- *Reveal* to him who You are and what Christ has done for him.
- *Open* the eyes of his understanding. Ephesians 1:18 Remove the spiritual blindness. 2 Corinthians 4:4
- *Draw* him to Yourself in a powerful fashion. John 6:44
- *Bind* Satan from him. Guard him from Satan stealing Your Word from him (Matthew 12:19).
- Pray for grace and mercy to *surround* him.
- Help *me* to be willing and anxious to be the means by which You save and deliver him. Lord, show me how to lead him to Christ.
- Send people across his path to bring him a witness of Christ.

Prayers for pastors and spiritual leaders

Biblical passages that can easily be used as prayers for pastors and leaders are Colossians 1:9-11; Philippians 1:9-11.

Pour out Your Spirit on (your pastor's name) and grant him:

- An overwhelming sense of Your presence
- Powerful conviction of sin
- A deep spiritual zeal and love for You
- The anointing, power and filling of the Spirit
- Clear discernment of Your will
- Deep purity and holiness
- A wall of protection from Satan's influence
- Abundant fulfillment of his personal and family needs
- Pure relationships and protect his marriage
- Fruitfulness in his ministry
- Pure motives

Twelve specific prayers for your church

- Pray for a powerful move of God's Spirit to bring deep conviction, repentance, and a mighty release of God's power.
- Pray for powerful anointing and direction upon our pastor and all teachers and church leaders. (Name them)
- Pray for deep love among members.
- Pray that strife and disunity will be subdued.
- Pray that Satan be completely bound from all the members and activities of the church.
- Pray for a strong wall of protection to surround the church and its members.
- Pray that the church will clearly receive God's direction in all decisions and ministries.
- Pray that the church clearly discerns God's vision for that particular congregation.
- Pray for a spirit of zeal in all ministries and initiatives.
- Pray for blessing and abundance of resources to do God's work.
- Pray for God to raise up many laborers for His work.
- Pray for a powerful spirit of worship, prayer and holiness to permeate the church.

Ten specific prayers for revival and spiritual awakening

(To be prayed for churches, cities and nations)

- Ask God to pour out deep conviction of sin, spiritual brokenness, a holy fear of God and genuine repentance among His people. There will be no revival without these elements and only

God can produce them in His people. After all, we cannot program or work up genuine brokenness and repentance (2 Corinthians 7:10).

- Pray for deep cleansing, genuine repentance, and spiritual power to engulf pastors and Christian leaders. Revival and spiritual awakening are extremely unlikely without a mighty move of God in pastors and Christian leaders. Renewed pastors are absolutely crucial to a move of God in our day (Ephesians 6:14-20).
- Pray for God to bestow spiritual hunger in His people and draw them to fervent intercession. God has to grant people the genuine faith and fervent desire for prayer. With all our prayer promotion and programming, we cannot "produce" a genuine prayer movement (Philippians 2:13).
- Pray that God will bring loving unity in our churches and a deep harmony between our churches. Many churches need healing among members and many churches need to stop competing jealously with other churches (John 13:35).
- Pray that God would fill His people with a passion to see people saved. (Only God can give a genuine burden for souls.) Until God's people intensely pray for the lost and do aggressive soul winning, revival will tarry. Be sure you are constantly praying for many lost people by name (Romans 9:1-3).
- Pray that God will give His people a passion for missions and starting churches. Great revivals produce an explosion of mission projects, new ministries, and new church starts. Only God can grant a genuine passion for missions (Matthew 28:19).
- Pray that God will call thousands into ministry, missions, and Christian service. Many churches are dying for lack of soul winners, teachers and church workers. Furthermore, we can start only as many churches as we have church planters to start them (Matthew 9:37).
- Pray that God will pour out His Spirit like a mighty purifying fire. Ask God to purify our "motives" as we pray for revival. It is possible to pray for revival for selfish or ambitious reasons. Our motives must be solely for: (a) the glory of God, and (b) the increase of the Kingdom of God. We must not pray for revival just to solve our own problems or make our church successful in the eyes of men (James 4:2).
- Pray for a mighty move of conviction and salvation to engulf major communities of cultural influence. Some key examples

are Hollywood actors and producers, government officials, educators, teachers, and college professors, news and media people, talk show hosts, comedians, homosexual activists groups, and music industry leaders (1 Timothy 2:1-2). Provide your congregation with specific lists of key people in each category.

- Specifically pray for God to pour out His Spirit in a fashion even greater than He did in America in 1858 and Wales in 1904. (Ten percent of Wales' population was saved in six months!) Ask God for a modern day of Pentecost in the United States and Canada (Mark 11:22-24; John 14:13-14).

Seven Specific Prayers for Local or National Elections

(without getting into politics) Based on principles from 1 Timothy 2:1-4

- Pray for people to seriously seek God in how they vote
- Pray that people will not put economics or politics above the godly and biblical foundations upon which America was founded
- Pray for God's Spirit to fill the voting booths and guide people as they vote
- Pray that huge numbers of godly people will turn out to vote
- Pray for people to follow God's guidance, not just political parties
- Pray that God will give us godly leaders of integrity who will govern in wisdom and righteousness
- Pray for God to have mercy on America and stay His hand of judgement

A Final Word About Intercession

The aforementioned prayers are examples of how God will lead you to specific intercession. As you meet with God, He will guide you in your own prayers and reveal biblical promises to claim before His throne. *It is especially important to combine your intercession with the biblical promises that God has quickened to your heart.*

Again, do not be overwhelmed by the potential depth of intercession. God will get you there one step at a time and at your own pace. True intercession represents the deepest and most sacrificial of all the types of prayer. By its very nature, intercession is sacrificial because it often focuses on people and issues that may not directly touch your life. But make no mistake — God has called *all* His children to some level of consistent intercession.

God has incredible blessings for all who embrace biblical levels of intercession. In our own church, we have seen scores of people saved by the simple intercession of a single evangelistic prayer group. There is no joy like seeing prayers consistently answered in the baptismal pool of your church! In the next chapter we examine the exciting subject of "hearing God's voice" though biblical meditation.

Questions for
Discussion and Reflection

1. How many of the fifteen basic intercession categories do you consistently lift to God?

2. When praying for the lost, list several scriptural words that should be part of our prayers.

3. List several specific requests you should pray for pastors and Christian workers. Why is it so important to pray biblically and specifically for our leaders?

4. List several biblical words you should pray for your church. Why is it so important to pray specifically?

5. List several biblical words you should pray for revival and spiritual awakening. Why must you learn to pray biblically and specifically?

Prayers for Daily Growth

* Father God, fill me with the spirit of genuine intercession. Help me stand in the gap for my land (Ezekiel 22:30).

* Lord God, as an intercessor teach my hands to war and my fingers to fight. Grow me up into powerful biblical prayers that spring from Your heart.

* Lord Jesus, forgive me for being lazy and inconsistent in the battle of intercession. Forgive me for praying general, non-specific prayers. Fill me with Yourself and teach me to allow Christ to pray through me.

Chapter Eight

Phase Five:
Hearing God's Voice Through Meditation

Meditation is a form of prayer because it is communication with God through prayerful listening. In meditation you are quietly listening for God's voice through His Word and the impressions He speaks to your heart. It is essential to remember that genuine prayer is a relationship and not just a habit or ritual. A genuine relationship requires *both* talking and listening.

There can be no real relationship unless it is two way. After all, how would you feel if your spouse talked all the time and never gave you a chance to speak? That would make for an extremely poor marriage and it also makes for a poor relationship with God! Meditation is that time when we specifically listen for God to speak to our heart.

Practical Guidelines for Daily Meditation

1. In your daily Bible reading, ask God to speak to your heart.

As you read God's Word, do not approach it as merely a book of history and doctrinal teachings. Though you should definitely research the context of the Scripture, you must approach the Bible as God's personal word to you on each new day. After reading a few verses you should pause and simply ask, "God, what are you saying to me?" In this way, prayer and Bible reading become powerfully inter-connected. This kind of reflective reading of Scripture will impact your prayer life immeasurably. God will personally speak to your heart!

2. When you have completed your daily time of Bible reading and prayer, write down key ideas and impressions.

I strongly urge you to keep a journal or notebook of your daily time with God. Keeping a personal journal or diary is one of the most powerful forms of meditation. A personal journal or spiritual diary helps facilitate a daily dialogue with God. A thorough personal journal is literally a written record of your relationship with God.

Another great advantage of journaling is that you form the habit of writing down the specific promises God reveals to your heart. When you actually record God's promises, you are much more likely to take them seriously. The written record becomes a source of great encouragement in future times of struggle.

Furthermore, writing down key thoughts and impressions helps you to get into a serious habit of *listening* for God's voice. Tragically, many people approach Bible reading and prayer without expecting to hear a personal word from God. We approach prayer as such a one-sided endeavor that we barely give God a chance to speak. So often we don't stop talking long enough for God to get a word in edge-wise!

3. Fill your life with the Word of God.

The more we are exposed to God's Word, the more He speaks to us and transforms our life. Surrounding yourself with God's Word is one variation of meditation. (Psalms 1:2 "In His law doth he meditate day and night.")

Today we are blessed with some innovative ways to be filled with God's Word. Some examples are: (a.) Playing tapes of Scripture reading while you drive, (b.) Playing music that is primarily made up of songs with Scripture lyrics, (c.) Participating in one of today's Scripture memorization programs, (d.) Placing framed Scriptures in strategic parts of your home or office. Deuteronomy 6:4-9 "Hear, O Israel: The Lord our God is one Lord: and thou shalt love the Lord thy God will all thine heart, and with all thy soul, and with all thy might. And these words, which I command thee this day, shall be in thine heart: and thou shalt teach them diligently unto thy children, and shalt talk of them when thou sittest in thine house, and when thou walkest by the way, and when thou liest down, and when thou risest up. And thou shalt bind them for a sign upon thine hand, and they shall be as frontlets between thine eyes. And thou shalt write them upon the post of thy house, and on thy gates."

The more we know and meditate on God's Word, the easier we will recognize His voice when He speaks. When you fill your life with Scripture, God revolutionizes your prayer life and your walk with Him!

4. When you pray, be sensitive to God's specific impressions through which He leads you to focus on various issues of concern.

At times, prayer and meditation intermingle as you sense God's unique promptings. Remember, your prayer time is not some pre-set formula that you mechanically follow each day. Some days God will lead you to spend much time in praise and little in confession. On other days, He may greatly burden you to intercede for specific people while focusing little on petition. "Likewise the Spirit also helpeth our infirmities; for we know not what we should pray for as we ought: but the Spirit itself maketh intercession for us with groanings which cannot be uttered" (Romans 8:26).

Though there will be a consistent balance in all the prayer types, at times God will give very unique promptings. Remember, God is to be in control and we must let Him guide our prayer time. Part of meditation is to pause in our praying and be sensitive to God's promptings. Friend, if this sounds too mysterious or difficult, please take heart. The more you spend time with God, the more you will learn to recognize His still small voice.

A Final Word About Meditation

In its essence, meditation is simply the practice of *listening* to God's voice as He speaks through His Word and prayer. It is this crucial element that makes our prayer life a two-way conversation rather than a one-way monologue. Meditation is the intentional act of listening to God. We must come to Bible study and prayer *expecting* to hear a personal word from a personal God.

I urge you not to let any of this seem overwhelming or complicated. Even if you feel weak in prayer, God will take you right where you are and do a mighty work in your life. Believe me, God is longing to speak to your heart in real and personal ways. I pray this chapter has made you hungry for something besides a one-way monologue with *you* doing all the talking! You will be amazed what you will hear when you take the time to listen!

Questions for
Discussion and Reflection

1. How biblical is your prayer life if you do all the talking?

2. Why does a healthy relationship with Christ require both talking and listening?

3. Describe four primary ways to hear God's voice through daily mediation.

Prayers for Daily Growth

* Lord, touch my ears so that I may hear Your voice. Anoint my eyes that I may see Yyour ways.

* Quicken my mind that every thought is captive to Christ (2 Corinthians 10:5). Touch my spirit daily with the revelation of Your Word.

* God, grant me a burning desire to daily hear Your voice by the revelation of the Word and prompting of the Holy Spirit.

A Brief Word About Fasting

(An excerpt from *Local Associations and United Prayer*)

Spirit-led fasting is one of the most neglected spiritual disciplines of our day. Perhaps this is a telling symptom of the "general luke-warmness" that characterizes much of American Christianity.

We are also a society that tends to emphasize instant, painless results in whatever we undertake. Beyond question, ours is a society that worships convenience and materialism. Quite simply, many today are in bondage to the flesh and are heavily influenced by fleshly appetites and desires. For this reason, to many, the idea of foregoing meals to pray and seek God seems very strange indeed. Brethren, this is a strong indication of just how desperately we need revival.

By no means am I suggesting fasting as a legalistic attempt to "earn revival" or somehow "impress God." That is most definitely not the purpose of fasting. However, the Bible clearly *assumes* that God's people will fast in their devotion to the Lord. The examples are numerous, but two have special relevance: 1) Joel 2:12-13 - "Now, therefore says the Lord, Turn to Me with all your hearts, With fasting, and weeping, and with mourning. So rend your heart, and not your garments; Return to the Lord your God, For He is gracious and merciful, Slow to anger, and of great kindness; And He relents from doing harm." 2) Matthew 6:16-18 - "Moreover, when you fast, do not be like the hypocrites, with a sad countenance. For they disfigure their faces that they may appear to men to be fasting. Assuredly, I say to you, they have their reward. But you, when you fast, anoint your head and wash your face, so that you do not appear to men to be fasting, but to your Father who is in the secret place; and your Father who sees in secret will reward you openly."

The Scriptures leave little doubt that God expects Spirit-led fasting to be a definite part of our relationship with Him. I sense this is an area in which God is increasingly dealing with His people. Especially at the pastors' prayer meetings and church or areawide nights of prayer, we are asking our people to prayerfully consider biblical fasting. Again, we are not promoting this in a heavy-handed or legalistic fashion.

Whether or not people actually fast should be a purely personal decision and something they do by the prompting of the Holy Spirit. Our pattern is to share the biblical concepts about fasting and then allow people to personally respond as God leads them. We encourage other associations to prayerfully consider how God may lead you in this area. An appropriate question to ask is: "How much are we really hungering for God Himself?"

For general guidance, I suggest the following points.

1. Ask God to enable you to fast by the leading of the Holy Spirit and *not* just because someone else fasted.

2. Fast with the purpose of turning aside from other things in order to more fully focus on God. (Do not fast merely as a ritual or some legalistic attempt to impress or manipulate God.)

3. Ask God to show you the type of fast He desires for you. There are many different types of fasting. Some examples are: (a) a complete fast for short periods, (b) water-only fasts, (c) juice fasts, (d) fasting from certain types of food, (e) fasting from certain activities or recreation. (Some of the most powerful fasting can be giving up favorite activities to spend intense time alone with God.)

4. The general biblical principle is not to publicize your fasting. We should avoid prideful boasting at all costs. (However, God may at times lead some to give testimony or write about this biblical element of prayer.)

5. Fasting is definitely connected with great urgency and power in prayer. Virtually all great awakenings were brought by prayer *and* fasting.

Beyond question, fasting is a basic biblical experience of our love relationship with Jesus Christ. Believer, is it not time for us to get serious about seeking God with all our hearts? May God guide us to genuine fasting that is fully willing to deny earthly appetites. May we experience a fast that is more than going without food. Let us pray that God will work into our hearts the glorious reality of Matthew 5:6, "Blessed are those who hunger and thirst for righteousness, For they shall be filled."

Chapter Nine

A Practical Daily Prayer Guide

In this final chapter I will outline a practical pattern for daily prayer. However, please understand this pattern is *not* some legalistic formula. Above all, your prayer time is a relationship and relationships fluctuate from day to day.

By no means are you required to always follow the exact order of this or any other pattern. Some days God may lead you to begin with confession and cleansing and actually end with praise and thanksgiving. At other times, God will lead you to spend far more time in intercession for others. On still other occasions, you may begin with quiet meditation and listening. Though the following format represents a powerful, biblical prayer pattern, it is not a rigid program. As you are sensitive to God's Spirit, He will guide you in a variety of patterns.

Friend, if you are serious about learning to pray, you will soon experience the most incredible journey of your life! Let us confidently claim God's glorious promise of Jeremiah 29:13. "And you shall seek Me, and find Me, when you shall search for Me with all your heart."

A Simple Pattern for Powerful Daily Prayer

I. Begin with a period of praise and thanksgiving (5-10 minutes)

    A. Give thanks for past, present, and future blessings

    B. Praise God for who He is (His characteristics and names)

    C. Freely worship and adore Him

II. Continue with confession and repentance (at least 5-10 minutes)

    A. Ask God to search your thoughts and attitudes

B. Carefully examine your speech

C. Ask God to thoroughly search your relationships

D. Confess any sins of commission and be sure to forsake the sins God reveals

E. Confess any sins of omission and make a definite commitment to obedience

F. Resolve to fully repent of any known sin of thought, word or deed

G. Ask God to fill you with the Holy Spirit

H. Be sure to utilize a thorough biblical tool designed to search all areas of your life with God's Word

III. Prayers of Personal Petition (10-15 minutes)

A. Pray for the development of character and holiness (Pray through the specific fruit of the Holy Spirit or other character words)

B. Pray for your ministry and service to God (be very specific in your prayers)

C. Pray for physical, emotional, spiritual or financial needs

IV. Prayers of Intercession (10-20 minutes)

A. Pray for needs of family and friends

B. Pray for your pastor and church (use specific prayers such as found on pages 84 and following)

C. Pray for specific lost people (use specific prayers such as found on page 83)

D. Pray for missionaries and mission efforts (use guides from the International Mission Board)

E. Pray for revival and spiritual awakening (use guides on page 84)

In your intercession, seek to be as specific as possible. Also remember the value of focusing on only two or three categories per day. If you thoroughly prayed for every category, you could literally pray for hours. Though some may be led to pray for hours, most people will be led to focus on certain categories on certain days. As always, the guiding principle is close sensitivity to the Holy Spirit.

V. Meditation and Assessment

A. Reflect on key points of your Scripture reading and prayer time

B. Assess what God has impressed to your heart

C. Write down key impressions in a daily journal

D. End your time with thanksgiving for God's presence.

Again, I emphasize the previous pattern is a general guideline, not a rigid program. As you allow God's Spirit to guide, you will be amazed at the ways He will direct you day by day.

It is awesome to pause and remember that Almighty God desires a close personal relationship with you. May God help us settle for nothing less than the glorious reality of His presence!

Points to Remember

In the above pattern, I did not specifically cover Bible reading. From previous chapters, I trust you already understand that daily Bible reading is essential to your prayer life. I suggest that you do your Bible reading and journaling before you conduct your main prayer time. I highly recommend that you follow one of today's excellent schedules for reading through the entire Bible at least once each year.

Let me also say I am not implying that you must pray a whole hour in order to experience a powerful prayer life. Though an hour is an excellent goal, it is not a requirement. It is certainly possible to experience significant prayer in shorter formats. If you are sensitive to God in your prayer time, you will have a life-changing experience whether it's thirty minutes or three hours! When people learn to truly encounter God in prayer, even hours in prayer can seem like a mere moment. May God help us settle for nothing less than a powerful relationship with Himself.

Conclusion

Beyond question, we live in a most strategic moment of history. Though our nation has never seen such moral decline, we are also witnessing a rising tide of prayer. We are now embroiled in a monumental spiritual war for the very souls of our society. Though the present battle is intense, I write with a glorious sense of hope (Philippians 1:6). I am convinced we are going to see worldwide revival and spiritual awakening of unprecedented proportions. (Even if it takes God's judgement to humble us!)

All around us, we see evidence God is preparing His Bride for the great marriage feast of the Lamb. Indeed, I believe the return of Christ may be at the very door! But regardless of the timing of His return, one thing is preeminent for every believer — the strength and vibrancy of your relationship to Christ!

God gave His only Son not just to get you into heaven, but to enable you to walk in miracle power and fruitful service (John 15:8). Friend, if you are saved your very birthright is mighty spiritual power and victory. And more than that, God wants to mightily use you for His Kingdom. Believer, it is vital that you now grow up and become a prayer warrior for God. You are a crucial part of His army and He is counting on you! He wants to use you in ways you can't even imagine. But all this ultimately hinges on one thing: the strength of your prayer life (John 14:12-14).

I am profoundly grateful you have read to the conclusion of this book on prayer. But in regards to prayer, I now implore you to become a "doer" and not a "hearer" only (James 1:22). In fact, you are now responsible to God for what you have read. Please don't settle for one more day with a mediocre prayer life or walk with Jesus. Don't settle for crumbs when God wants you to experience a feast of His presence and power. Dear friend, if you will commit to significant daily time with God, not even the sky is the limit to what He will do in your life (Ephesians 3:20).

A Prayer of Commitment

* Father God, help me be satisfied with nothing less than all of Yourself. Save me from mere prayer ritual that I may walk in holy worship, genuine obedience and the glorious fullness of Your Son. May Your glory and pleasure be my only cause.

SDG